To : Paul

From: Peter, Christine,
Stephen and Laura

Happy Tackling!
Christmas 1987

BRYAN ROBSON'S
SOCCER
SKILLS

Edited by **Tom Tyrrell**

Specially commissioned
photographs by
Peter Robinson
Official FIFA photographer

HAMLYN

Acknowledgements

Photographs
Front jacket: Associated Sport
Back jacket: Peter Robinson/International Sports Book Network
All photographs by Peter Robinson/International Sports Book Network
except the following:
Steve Hale/International Sports Book Network: pages 10 (all), 11 (all);
photograph reproduced from *United I Stand* by Bryan Robson, published by
Pelham Books Limited, 1984: 123; Bob Thomas Sports Photography: 15 top, 51 top

Artwork Leigh Jones

The author and publisher would like to thank Manchester United Football Club
for their invaluable help before and during the photographic sessions, particularly:
Players: Russell Beardsmore, Deiniol Graham, Jimmy O'Donnell,
Mark Robins, David Scott, Phil Steer, David Wilson
Old Trafford staff: kit manager: Norman Davies; groundsman: Gordon Loughmane; laundry: Sharon Walker; Nora Whalley

Published by
The Hamlyn Publishing Group Limited
Bridge House, 69 London Road
Twickenham, Middlesex TW1 3SB, England
and distributed for them by
Octopus Distribution Services Limited
Rushden, Northamptonshire NN10 9RZ, England

First published in 1987

ISBN 0 600 55211 X

Printed in Italy

CONTENTS

INTRODUCTION

I really can't remember when I wasn't playing soccer. Ever since I've been able to walk I've always wanted to kick a ball around, and I've been lucky to have had years of enjoyment doing just that.

But like almost every professional I love the game, and I've always been prepared to make sacrifices to improve my standards.

When I was a schoolboy I thought there was nothing better than getting along to the local playing field with my pals – after doing my homework – and playing soccer for a couple of hours. It didn't matter about equipment; we had a ball, some makeshift goals and a game called soccer.

You probably do the same sort of thing yourself. Perhaps you're in your school team, or play for the local youth club. Maybe you're hoping to be a professional yourself one day, or play at senior level for a local amateur side.

It doesn't really matter what your target is as long as you get pleasure out of a game which gives enjoyment to millions every week. Whether you play or watch I think it's important that you have some knowledge of soccer skills, and throughout the pages of this book I've tried to pass on some of my knowledge and experience to you.

That includes some basic tactics and a big chunk on fitness and training – in my mind a vital area of the game too often overlooked.

My intention has been to create a book which can be used to help you get some idea of the correct way to develop your skills, understand tactics, improve your strength and fitness . . . and enjoy your soccer.

My message to coaches is simple: let the players get pleasure out of the game. My message to you is: have fun playing soccer, the greatest game in the world.

Bryan Robson

USING YOUR FEET

Leave the circus tricks alone until you've made it to the top grade. It's all right being able to catch the ball on the back of your neck and roll it round your shoulders, but you can't do it during a game. Get the basics right and the tricks can come afterwards

Let's start by getting right down to basics . . . kicking a ball. It's the one element of soccer that makes it so different from any other sport. The majority of ball games are played with the hands, or with something held in the hands, but association football is just what it says it is – a game played with the feet.

That makes your feet the most important weapons in your armoury.

Not only do your feet move you around the field of play and carry you into position, but they also act as your means of winning the ball, keeping possession, taking control, passing to a colleague, and of course shooting for goal to score. So the foot comes first.

Kicking a ball sounds simple and it is simple. It's something that almost everyone must have done at some time in their lives, yet I think I'm pretty safe in saying that the vast majority of people won't have kicked a ball properly. This could be one of the main reasons that they never get the best possible enjoyment out of their football.

Give a small child a ball and he or she will most probably kick it with their toes, or at least the toe-end of their shoe. Not so long ago soccer boots were made with a solid toe-cap, which gave the impression that this was the kicking point of the boot – but it's not so; you should never kick the ball with your toes.

Imagine you're on a beach barefooted. You're playing soccer with a group of friends when the ball comes to you. It's only a light plastic ball, yet if you kick it with your toes it will hurt. Your toes get pushed back and the ball can fly off in any direction.

Put on a pair of soccer boots, substitute a real soccer ball for the lightweight plastic version and the result is the same. So toes are out, except in an emergency.

The inside of the foot

Whether I'm kicking the ball one yard or twenty yards I would always use the inside of the foot if possible. It's the most simple action in the game, propelling the ball along the ground in the direction you want it to go.

Using the inside of the foot gives the kicker the

Right. Using the inside of the foot for a low accurate kick.

Far right. Kicking with the instep.

ROBSON'S TIPS

● *Look after your feet – keep them clean and make sure that your toenails are trimmed regularly. Nails that are too long or too short can cause you problems.*

● *Always wear boots that feel comfortable. They shouldn't be too tight or over-sized, letting your feet slip out of them.*

● *When kicking the ball keep your eye on it all the time; don't lift your head up at the last moment. Sense where the target is, but watch the ball and you will add accuracy to your kicking.*

● *The non-kicking leg is as important as the kicking one. Get the non-kicking foot alongside the ball whenever possible. This gives you better balance and helps you to control the ball on contact. If your non-kicking leg is too far behind the ball you will over-stretch, and if you get too far beyond the ball balance and contact will be affected and you will lose power and distance.*

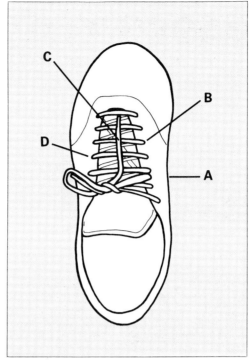

Kicking areas of the foot: **A** The inside: Used for playing accurate low passes or placing the ball in a specific spot. **B** The instep: The most used kicking zone. Chips, crosses, shots of any length can be made with the instep. **C** The top: The most powerful contact area. A ball driven with the top of the foot will travel with maximum force. This area is used when volleying at goal or clear of trouble. **D** The outside: A bending volley, a curving chip or a ball controlling area – that is the role of the outside of the foot. (Note this is an illustration of a left foot. For the right foot all areas are on the opposite side.)

best control of both the direction and speed of the ball, and it's a simple skill to practise using one foot then the other, tapping the ball to a friend or up against a wall.

The instep
Now if you imagine your foot as an arch, flat at the bottom and rounding up to a steady curve, then dropping down to the base again, you can quickly find the next kicking surface.

The inside of the foot is the flat part of the wall; above it, before you reach the top of the arch, is the instep, running along a line from your big toe towards your ankle bone on the inside of your leg. This gives you a more powerful kicking area, letting you drive a pass and lift the ball, increasing the distance of your kicking.

When kicking a ball with the instep you have a better chance of extending your follow-through, carrying the kick on along the line of the ball, and this gives you accuracy as well as extra distance.

Kicking with the inside of the foot means that the action is more of a short stab. You can't really follow through very much using this method, because you've turned your knee outwards and leg movement is restricted. Using the instep gives the leg a longer swinging area.

The top of the foot
The third kicking zone is the top of the foot, the peak of the arch I described earlier.

This is the power zone, the shooting area. This is the part of the foot which gives you the firmest point with which to hit the ball. You can use it to

send the ball downfield to pick out a colleague, to clear danger from your own goalmouth or to volley a shot at goal. Obviously because you have taken the point of impact to the crest of the curved arch you may not have total control and the ball can be misdirected.

The outside of the foot
The outside of the foot lets you bend the flight of the ball. It's difficult to kick the ball straight when using the outside of the foot, because at some point of its flight it will start to curve, but this can be used to good effect with practice to bend a pass away from an opponent.

The kicking action used in making contact with the outside of the foot means that you are slicing the ball. You can make contact with the middle of the ball, but your leg is passing on a line off centre. Therefore the ball will be spinning as it leaves the foot and this curves its flight.

So there we have the four main contact areas: inside, instep, top and outside. Each separate type of kick must be developed if you want to improve your game.

You can of course kick the ball with your heel – and the backheel is a useful addition to your skills. It could be a little flick back to a colleague as an opponent challenges, or a sharp kick to the side using the heel of your kicking leg as it passes across the front of your standing leg, even a snapshot near goal. But it's not a major contact area.

Once you can kick a ball with confidence the method you use for each aspect of your game will come naturally and will help you enjoy your game even more.

PASSING

❝ To me a good player is one who can pick out a colleague with a pass over any distance. If 9 times out of 10 he can pass the ball accurately over anything from 5 to 50 yards he's well on the way to success ❞

1 Accurate passing is vitally important to your game. Here I make sure that the ball reaches a colleague by kicking it straight to his feet, using the inside of the foot to keep the ball low.

2 I time my pass to give the best advantage. By waiting for the opponent to come close it makes interception more difficult and I can pick out my unmarked team mate.

3 The way to my team mate is blocked momentarily by an opponent, but I can still pass to him by playing the ball into an area wide of the marker and close enough for him to run on to.

4 Two players against one often happens, and here the opponent is in two minds who to cover. He moves towards me and I'm able to time my pass to give us the best advantage.

5 My team mate picks up the pass as he runs forward. A return ball played to me, past another opponent, would be a 'wall pass' giving the same effect as kicking a ball at a wall and collecting it on the rebound.

Soccer is a team game and the accurate pass is one of the most essential ball skills. It's no use being able to flick the ball from foot to foot, flick it up in the air and catch it on the back of your neck if you can't pick out a colleague with a 30-yard pass.

I've always felt that juggling with a ball is better left to the circus act unless you've reached the very top of the grade in soccer. Until then your game can be improved in many other areas, and one of the most vital is passing.

A well-timed ball played to a colleague can open up chances in a game, and the difference between a good team and a bad one is usually down to the number of good passes which they make.

If you watch a Saturday morning game between a group of young boys you'll usually find that each individual will try to do too much during the action. One boy will hold the ball, others will try to take it from him, and the game will resemble a swarm of bees buzzing round a honey-pot . . . the honey-pot being the ball.

The pass stops all that. The idea of the pass is to give the ball to a team-mate who is in a better position than you are to do something positive with it. You might be attacking goal or in a defensive crisis, but either way a good pass can make all the difference.

You get very little time to think during a game of soccer, and the higher the level you reach the quicker you have to be to outwit an opponent, because you can bet that they're trying their best to read your thoughts and anticipate the next move.

The pass should give your colleague a chance to get the ball under control and use it well. The passer should be looking for the best place to direct the ball, the receiver should be ready to get to that spot and carry on the move.

The most accurate method for the short pass is the kick along the ground with the inside of the foot, and a pass to feet is the most basic. The ball is sent from the passer to the receiver's feet as he approaches, but it can also be played 'short', especially if you know that your colleague has the speed to beat the man who may be marking him.

Passing into space

Another effective short pass is to direct the ball into space beyond an opponent, in the direction your team-mate is running. To time your pass so that the ball reaches the point which is the most advantageous to your team means that passing must be practised as much as any other area of skills.

A well-timed pass can win a game, and the team that can move the ball from player to player and keep possession is going to have a better chance of victory than all those bees round the honey-pot!

Develop your passing in the same way as your basic kicking. Start with the short pass and work your way up towards the day when you can place the ball into the path of a team-mate half a pitch away and you'll be well on the way to success.

6 The chipped pass is an effective way of beating an opponent while picking out a colleague with the ball.

7 The way is blocked by an opponent, but by chipping the ball over his head I'm able to play a longer pass for a team mate to collect.

8 The ball's on its way and there's little the opponent can do to intercept.

ROBSON'S TIPS

● *Until you're confident of making an accurate pass you're wasting your time developing other areas of your game. Working on passing the ball is vital. Try to practise the pass whenever you can find the time.*

● *The sidefoot pass is the simplest pass in the game. Practise getting the ball to a colleague's feet, then concentrate on timing your pass so that the ball arrives on the spot your team-mate wants it at the moment he can make best use of the ball.*

● *Using the inside of the foot allows you to send the ball along the ground into the path of a team-mate while shielding it from an opponent who is coming from behind.*

● *Don't try long passes until you've mastered the technique of playing the ball accurately over a short distance.*

THE LONG BALL

‘ You'll find with practice you can kick the ball further with either your instep or the outside of your foot. You're driving the ball to get distance so your timing has got to be spot on; the kick should be at its most powerful point as you strike the ball, but the follow-through will keep it on course and add distance ,

Kicking the ball over a long distance is vitally important to the development of your game. Obviously nobody expects a young child to be able to kick the ball the full length of the field, but at the same time youngsters should practise playing the ball over increasing lengths of the field as they grow in strength and confidence.

Short-pass practice can be lengthened by a few yards at first. Then, when this distance is achieved consistently, the area covered can be extended further.

Kicking the ball a long way means that the contact foot is going to have to meet the ball in one of three ways – the instep, the top of the foot or the outside. The foot is going to have to swing under the ball, the toes tucking under the bottom curve of the ball as it meets the ground leaving the point of impact clear to make contact with the centre of the ball.

But the right position of the head and the standing leg, as well as the knee of the kicking leg is essential in any method of kicking.

The head is as important as the foot when kicking a ball. In order to get direction, power and distance the head should be over the ball and you must look at the ball as you kick it. It's no use lifting your head up at the last minute or you'll take your eye off the ball and miss it, or at least make a hash of what you're trying to do.

The 'dead' ball

Kicking a 'dead', or stationary, ball over a long distance – whether it's from a goal kick, a free kick or a corner – requires a combination of the skills just mentioned.

Your standing leg must be alongside the ball. This gives you the correct position from which to swing the striking leg and follow through without losing your balance.

The striking foot has got to kick *through* the ball, the point of contact being made with the ball as the toe passes under it. It's also crucial that the kicking leg follows through the action: stopping sharply will not add anything to either distance or direction, and you will simply lose your rhythm.

Some powerful kickers can punch the ball great distances with very little backswing or follow-through, but this is a skill which can be developed only *after* the basic technique of the long kick has been mastered.

The long ball introduces a new concept to your game. You are able to switch play from wing to wing, to clear the ball away from your half of the field and put the opposition under pressure, to

float a cross over the heads of defenders and pick out a colleague coming in on the blind side, to take free kicks and corners with confidence.

To be able to kick a ball over a reasonable distance is important to every player. Defenders can ease pressure and start attacking moves, midfielders can pick out someone in a forward position, and strikers can have a pot shot at goal from outside the penalty area.

Obviously if you're able to take an accurate free kick from anything over 25 yards – less for youngsters – you're going to be able to threaten your opponents, and the same kicking method for the long ball should be used, the objective being to keep the ball on target while maintaining power.

The moving ball

Kicking the ball a longer distance when it's already off the ground is simpler. The ball may have reached you after being played through the air by another player, or it could have been thrown into your path. To get distance with your kick you have to make sure that you get the non-kicking leg into a position alongside the ball, even though it's still moving.

To do this you must time your moment of contact so that you arrive in a kicking position at the precise second that the ball should be kicked. Early arrival of the striking foot will send the ball high into the air, while late arrival will mean lack of distance.

It's all to do with timing – and practice. Throwing a ball down in front of you and meeting it with a volley is a simple way of learning to kick over long distances. Taking free kicks from the halfway line and trying to direct the ball into the penalty area is another good exercise, and one which can be practised in a group.

ROBSON'S TIPS

● *Don't just run out onto the practice ground and boot the ball blindly downfield. Build up distance as you improve accuracy.*

● *Remember that kicking a ball over any distance is not simply a question of brute force. Your timing has got to be correct, plus the positioning of your head, body and non-kicking foot.*

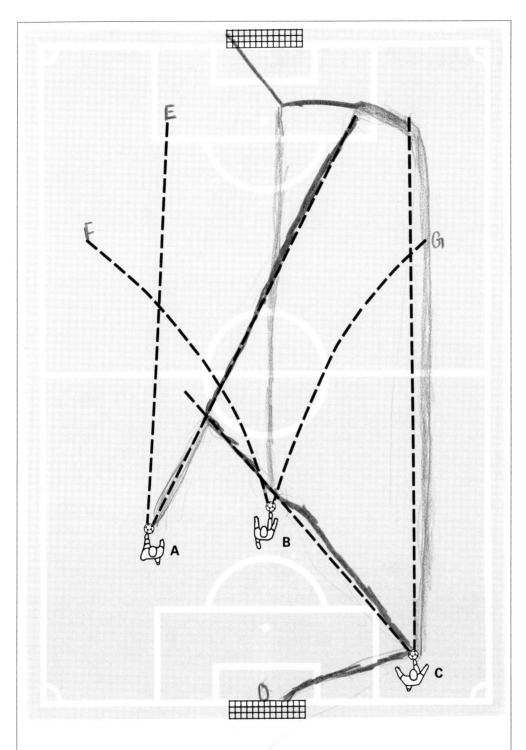

Using the long ball: **A** A player out wide on the left of the defence can use the long ball to send his winger forward or play diagonally across field to switch play. **B** From central midfield the long ball to either wing is a good method of changing play. **C** The right full-back can play a long ball in front of his attacker by kicking over the heads of the advancing defenders or by using a similar length ball to a wide midfield player on the left and cutting out the threat from the opposing midfielders.

▬ ▬ Path of ball

VOLLEYING

❝ The slightest backward movement of the body when kicking the ball on the volley will send it high into the air. You've got to concentrate on the ball, with no distractions at all, and keep watching it onto your foot so that you can get your timing exactly right. It's the old secret of any ball game . . . keep your eye on the ball ❞

The driven volley is the most powerful method of kicking the ball, because the kicker can make such 'clean' contact compared with a shot off the ground. The volley means that both the ball and the foot are moving at the time of contact, so timing is a vital part of this kicking skill.

The power volley at goal requires contact with the top of the foot, the drive area, while the long volley to a colleague is carried out by making contact with the instep. It's also possible to volley the ball with both the inside and outside of the foot, although a ball played with the inside would be more of a lob than an orthodox volley.

When volleying it's essential that you get yourself into a position similar to that being used when kicking a stationary ball.

You've got to keep your head and your knee well over the top of the ball, and this way you'll send it in the direction you're aiming towards and keep it reasonably low. Lean back and the ball goes higher; if you're not over the ball when you make contact it can fly off anywhere.

The high volley

Sometimes a ball will come to you above knee height, and your only chance of making good contact is to lean over on your non-kicking leg, and swing your striking foot at the ball.

By dipping the shoulder that's opposite your kicking foot (the right shoulder for a left-footed kick, or the left shoulder for a right-footed volley), you're still keeping your head over the ball, but from an angle.

Your head, shoulders and leg have stayed in a straight line. Your standing leg may have left this line but your point of contact is the same – below your head with the kicking knee directly above the ball at the point the foot makes contact with it.

Right: When volleying you must follow the flight of the ball with your eyes and time your kick to make contact in the area where you will get maximum power. Here the ball is leaving my foot after impact but my eyes still follow the flight.

Far right: The follow-through, an essential part of each method of ball contact.

With this volley I completed a hat-trick for England against Turkey in Istanbul – the first of my international career.

The half-volley

The half-volley doesn't mean that you kick the ball half as powerfully as you would do for a volley. In fact you get almost as much out of this type of kick as you do from the full volley.

The half-volley is a favourite shot in tennis, timing the swing of the racquet so that it makes contact with the ball a split-second after it bounces. Technically I suppose that there's no such thing as a half-volley, because the ball is just beginning its upward bounce from the ground as you make contact, so if you could photograph the shot at high speed it would probably turn out to be a volley!

But we've come to accept the half-volley as another part of a soccer player's skills, and its execution is fairly straightforward.

It's a favourite method of goalkeepers for kicking the ball downfield. From the normal volley (punt) they tend to get height in their clearance kicks, but from a half-volley, when the foot makes contact with the ball just at the moment when it hits the ground, the kick will stay lower and can often go further.

During a game a ball will come to a player in the air many times. He sometimes has the choice of volleying it, knowing that he may lose accuracy, or hitting it on the half-volley, but his timing must be perfect to get the best results.

As for any kick the head must be over the ball, the knee of the kicking leg above the point of contact and the foot in position to strike the ball in the required manner. The standing leg has to be brought alongside the ball, and if all the ingredients are used correctly the volley and half-volley will be carried out to perfection.

Below left: The height of the ball means that the best contact can be made only by jumping into the flight. I prepare for take-off.

Below centre: Both feet are off the ground for the volley but I'm still watching the ball up to the point of contact.

Below right: Landing after contact, still keeping an eye on the ball.

BENDING THE FLIGHT

‚ When you see a Brazilian player bending a 25-yard free kick round the keeper into the roof of the net you must realize that it's not a matter of luck. It takes skill and practice to perfect a spectacular shot. But the atmosphere can also play a part in the flight of the ball, and on a cold wet afternoon in the winter you aren't going to get that many 25-yard benders! ‚

Bending the flight of the ball is one of the most effective methods of causing problems for the opposition. You can use a curling kick from a corner and 'pull' the goalkeeper off his line chasing a floated cross which drifts out of his reach, or put defenders in all sorts of panic if you curl one the other way so that the ball flies towards the goal.

You can bend the ball with the outside of the foot, or if you want it to swing the other way, kick it with the inside of the foot, using the same principle for either kick.

The idea is to kick half the ball: slicing the ball puts spin into it and the spin makes it curve.

Now kicking half a ball may sound difficult, but imagine that the ball is in fact a flat circle rather than a sphere. The idea behind bending the flight is to get your foot to pass through the circle on either side of the central dividing line.

If you kick straight down the central line the ball will travel in a straight line, but if you kick it off-centre it will leave the foot on a curved arc spinning in flight and moving in the direction of the spin.

Once again the simple kicking techniques come into play. You have to concentrate on the area of the ball with which you're going to make contact, get your head, body and legs into the correct position and time your kick well.

We all know that the Brazilians have made the swerving shot world famous since they made its reputation in the World Cup in Mexico in 1970 when for the first time we saw the ball bending this way and that . . . and many people forget that the atmosphere has a lot to do with the way the ball travels.

Playing at altitude in Mexico you can kick the ball far greater distances than you can at or near sea level, and playing in a hot country where the air is warm inside and outside the ball will make it do things that perhaps it doesn't normally do in a colder climate. Combine atmosphere and altitude with the super skills of the Brazilians and the unstoppable free kicks come into the game.

I've often noticed when I've played in a hot country, or even on a very hot day in England, that the ball will bend more than it does in winter, and that is probably the most significant reason why the 'Brazilian bender' isn't a regular feature of the English game.

Short-range free kicks, those just outside the penalty area, can be very effective if the kicker can swerve the ball. There's nothing more worrying for a goalkeeper than to see a player with a reputation for swerving free kicks, lining up to take a shot at goal from 20 yards out. Which way will it bend? Only the kicker knows as he runs up to strike the ball.

'Draw' and 'fade'

Let's go back to our flat circle – a slice taken out of the centre of the ball with a dividing line running from top to bottom.

To bend a shot at goal using the inside of the foot, a right-footed kicker would kick at the right side of the ball approaching it from the left and striking to the right of centre in the bottom half of the ball.

The ball will curve away to the right as it leaves the foot, returning to the target area left of the kicker. It's the sort of movement golfers refer to as 'drawing' the ball, pulling it back to target after apparently aiming off to the right.

The opposite of the 'draw' is the 'fade' which in effect is a controlled slice, the ball setting off on a line to the left of target then curving back to the right.

By striking the left of the ball with the outside of the foot, the right-footed kicker slices through a line which is off-centre. The flight is the reverse of that created by using the inside of the foot.

Kicking a bending shot from a stationary ball requires a great deal of skill and practice, but there are other opportunities to try a 'bender' during a game and they can be put to good effect.

ROBSON'S TIPS

● *When bending a shot you're kicking across the back of the ball so your follow-through will not be in line with the target.*

● *An outswinging corner can cause just as many problems as one which swerves towards goal because the keeper may not be able to judge its flight path.*

● *Don't try to bend the ball until you've completely mastered kicking it straight. Be sure that you know the correct kicking techniques and practise striking the ball firmly with the instep or outside of the foot to discover which angle of approach and contact gives you the greatest amount of swerve.*

Bending the volley

The sliced volley uses the same principles as before, the foot passing across the back of the ball to make contact. For a player who is standing in the centre of the shooting zone it gives three areas of approach to the target.

I'm naturally left-footed and if a ball was dropping towards me outside the penalty area I might decide that my best scoring chance would lie in a swerving shot using the outside of my left foot.

To do this I'd get into position with my right leg alongside the ball, and hit across the back of the ball with my left. I'd make contact with the bottom right 'quarter' of the ball with my foot travelling on a line that was off to the right of the target. The ball would then curve back in from the right — and the fact that I had volleyed it would give it the extra power needed perhaps to beat the goalkeeper.

If I'd struck the ball with the instep of my left foot the approach would have been reversed: the follow-through would be to the left of the target and the flight in to the right from the left.

The third option would of course have been a volley direct at the target.

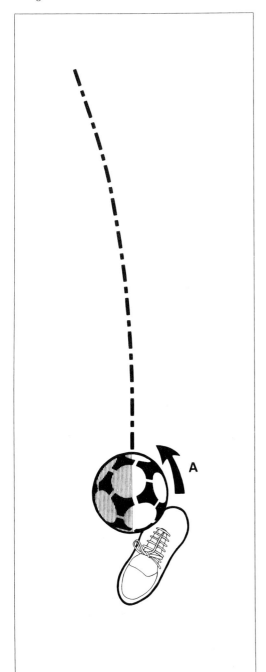

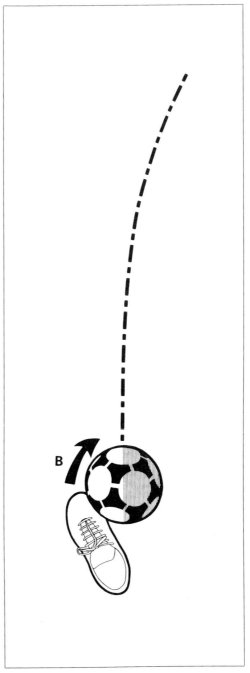

Kicking through half the ball to bend the flight: To bring the ball in from the right **A** the foot passes through the right hand half of the ball. The opposite applies when 'fading' a kick into the target. **B**: the kick is through the left side to impart a clockwise spin on the ball. In both cases the ball should fly fairly straight before curling in on the desired path.

CHIPPING AND CROSSING

❝ There's nothing more frustrating for a tall defender than an opponent chipping the ball over his head to pass to a colleague. There's a good chance the defender might even go for the ball with his hands, and if he's in the penalty area . . . **❞**

The chip in soccer is about as versatile as the deep-fried version! Chips with everything can really apply to the game of soccer because a chipped ball can be used as a pass, a way of beating an opponent, a means of rescuing in defence, or beating the goalkeeper in attack.

Yes, the chip is a useful skill to develop – and it takes us right back to the first approaches to the game for its introduction.

The chip can be carried out with the inside of the foot, the instep, the top of the foot or the outside. It's a delicate kick which is very controlled in its execution so that contact with the ball is not too forceful.

One way of practising the chip is to find an area about the size of a tennis court (a court is ideal if you can use one) and with a colleague simply kick the ball over the net allowing it to bounce once before returning it.

The chip then becomes a natural part of the exercise, one bounce and then return, using first the inside of the foot, then the instep and, as the game progresses, the top and outside of the foot.

The ball is lobbed in its flight, dropping over the obstacle and into the path of your team-mate. Substitute an opponent for the net and increase the height, and you have the principle of the chip – to lift the ball off the ground over a reasonably short distance.

I know it sounds as if I'm back in the kitchen again, but chips can be long or short . . . and it all depends on the backlift and follow-through.

The aim is to strike the bottom of the ball, the toes passing underneath as contact is made with the lower part of the instep. This lifts the ball quickly and puts backspin on it so that when it lands it won't bounce forward very far.

It's the same for both a moving or a dead ball: a stabbing movement with the kicking foot, a short backlift and virtually no follow-through.

Chipping over an advancing goalkeeper is a very effective method of scoring if it's a case of you or the keeper and the ball which floats over the heads of a defensive wall when they're expecting a fierce shot can create a real chance for your alerted colleagues.

Crossing the ball

An extension of the chip is the cross, a ball played through the air but over a greater distance, and here the striking area of the foot stays the same but the backlift and follow-through are extended to give more power.

If I'm crossing a ball on the run I push it into position and strike it firmly on the lower side making sure that my foot travels underneath it as I make contact.

But if I'm taking a corner and wanting to drive the ball to the far post then I just kick straight through the middle of the ball, getting my foot in a position which enables me to make contact with the top of the boot.

Once more I have to emphasize the necessity of concentrating on the area of the ball you're going to kick – and making sure that your technique is correct.

Right: Crossing the ball needs a positive approach to give you acceleration and power at the point of contact.

Centre right: Kicking over any distance requires a higher backlift of the striking leg to give you power as you kick through the ball.

Far right: Contact is made with the instep as the toes pass under the bottom of the ball, forcing it off the ground.

ROBSON'S TIPS

● *If you 'stab' at a ball moving towards you it'll fly into the air with backspin. It's a useful trick for beating an advancing opponent.*

● *Instead of slamming the ball into the defensive wall at a free kick, approach as if you were about to take a normal kick, then chip over the defenders into the space behind them.*

● *Remember that if a goalkeeper is running at you he'll have no chance of getting to a ball chipped over his head, especially if he's been drawn to the edge of the penalty area.*

Crossing isn't an easy skill for beginners, partly because of the distances involved and partly because you're kicking a different way from the direction you're going. The key is not to be too ambitious: practise your long kicking and your short crosses, and soon you'll find they come together.

Top right: The approach for the chip is almost identical to that used for the long cross, but the follow-through is shorter.

Centre right: I lean back slightly to give the kick more loft and my studs take a divot from the turf as my kicking foot passes through the ball.

Bottom right: The follow-through for the chip is a short step across the supporting leg.

SHOOTING

❝ The player you have to worry about most in front of goal is the one who has developed his all-round skills to such an extent that you can't predict his next move, a player who can control the ball quickly, shoot with precision – and doesn't waste time thinking what he's going to do ❞

I've been dealing with basics so far and we've reached the point where I focus on the main aim behind a game of soccer, to score goals. Shooting is a skill which, while it needs hours of practice to develop, really requires only the use of the kicking techniques already covered plus a new one – quick thinking.

To score goals means you have to outwit your opponents, get yourself into an advantageous position and hit the target.

To be able to shoot you have to have confidence in your kicking ability, and that's why when you practise any kicking skill it's always ideal if you can use some sort of target. You can aim for circles drawn on a wall, a patch of grass that stands out from other parts of the field, or simply kick in the direction of whoever it is you are practising with. Accuracy is essential and power comes next.

Once you've mastered the technique of kicking the ball with the basic methods you can turn your attention to scoring goals, and any of the front

foot methods can bring you goals. You can of course score with a backheel, but this doesn't really fall under the heading of 'shooting'.

A shot is a well-struck kick at goal. It can be a volley, or a half-volley, hit with the inside, instep, top or outside of the foot. For sheer power the top

of the foot is number one: toes down, non-kicking leg alongside the ball as it reaches the striking position, head over the ball.

You may find that you haven't got the time to position yourself for the type of kick that you'd most like to use. An opponent is bearing down on you, the ball has been sent in your direction and you have to get a shot in. It's no use standing there thinking, 'I'll use the inside of my right foot for this one,' since that opportunity might not come along. Go for the ball and hit it at goal; your natural kicking skill will help you make the best strike. Provided you have confidence that you can kick the ball firmly when making contact, that is enough to make you a threat in front of goal.

Shooting techniques

Each one of the kicking techniques will project the ball at goal, and each one offers something different to the kicker.

The inside of the foot will direct the ball along the ground and will give you the chance of placing the ball in a particular area of the goal. It's ideal if the goalkeeper has come off his line, the goalmouth is empty and you know that all that's needed is for you to be on target. At times like this to swing your leg blindly at the ball might simply send it flying off in any direction; a cool, sharply hit inside-foot shot is a winner every time.

The instep kick adds power. A ball arriving from your right as you face goal with your body towards the far post and your left shoulder

---

ROBSON'S TIPS

● *A fiercely hit volley might look spectacular, but if the way to goal is blocked a delicate chip can more easily bring the right results.*

● *Shooting is simply an extension of any basic kicking method. The volley, half-volley, sidefoot, instep, inside foot and the top of the foot are all part of shooting, but the essential ingredient is instinct: knowing where the goal is and going for it.*

---

pointing to the left of the near post presents you with the perfect position for using the instep of your right foot. But you must watch the ball – you know where the goal is and have a picture in your mind of where your opponents are standing as you make contact, and the instep kick gives you the power to put a strong shot on target.

The outside of the foot will curve your shot. From the right of the target you must remember that you want the ball to curl into goal and therefore strike in the correct area (see bending the flight).

Below left: Eyes on the ball, non-striking leg alongside, I lift back my kicking leg as part of my running stride.

Below centre: The shot is on its way.

Below right: My kicking leg follows the flight and my eyes stay on the ball.

THE OTHER FOOT

> ❛ You shouldn't just use your better, 'natural' foot. If you can develop ball skills with both feet you're doubling your value to the team ❜

Below left: The running backheel. I step over the ball to strike it with the heel of my left foot.

Below centre: Contact – the ball is on its way to a colleague coming up from behind.

Below right: I continue my run, giving a teammate the chance to pick up my pass as I draw an opponent.

So far I've dealt with what you could describe as the basic techniques of kicking a ball, using the kicking areas of the front of the foot to send the ball in various directions and in a variety of ways. Now I'd like to turn to the 'other foot'.

That may come as a surprise to many of you, especially if you use the other foot in the same manner as you use your 'natural' kicking foot. But so many people, even some very famous players, have been 'one-footed'; in other words they so prefer kicking the ball with their natural kicking foot they forget they have a 'spare' on the end of their other leg!

If you're naturally left-footed, as I am, practise using your right until it becomes easy for you to kick the ball with that foot too. Start with the basics, tapping the ball against a wall, but using the foot you don't normally favour. The more you practise using both feet the more your game will broaden.

Kicking with the inside of the foot is perhaps the simplest way to start to develop the use of your weaker leg. The action is straightforward enough and is simply a mirror of the technique used when you kick with your stronger leg.

The most important thing to remember is that you must position yourself properly. If you're naturally right-footed, and whenever you approach a kick you make sure that your left leg is alongside the ball, then when you're using the other foot it's the right leg that's got to be placed

correctly to support your body weight as you make contact.

It's a fairly common sight when someone is trying to develop their kicking action on their weak side to see that they instinctively prepare themselves to kick the ball with their stronger leg, then suddenly change feet to put their stronger leg alongside the ball and make a complete mess of the contact.

The thing to remember is to take your time. If

you rush into anything there's every chance you will fail, so start 'weak leg' practice with the inside of the foot: firm stance, head over the ball, plenty of concentration and a confident strike.

Once you've found out how easy it is then the next step is to develop another kicking action with your weaker leg.

Dropping a ball just in front of you enables you to get the feel of a kick with the outside of the foot and the top of the boot making sure that you time your kick to make contact while the ball is still off the ground, just a few inches away from a bounce.

By making contact in this way you can get used to swinging your weaker leg at the ball, adjusting your balance on your normal kicking leg and making sure that your head and body are in the right position.

The next step is to kick a stationary ball, driving it short distances at first and then building up to longer kicks as confidence grows.

Getting two 'strong' sides

Being able to kick with either foot is an obvious advantage because you won't have a 'weak side' which can be attacked by an opponent quick to spot that you have to put the ball on a particular side before you can kick it. You can very easily be forced into positions where you can't play the ball if you haven't a hope of kicking it with your weaker leg.

Goalkeepers also take note. If you always take kicks from the hands with your right leg, try kicking a few with your left. Develop the long kick with either foot and you'll see what a difference it makes to your game.

I beat the West German defence and prepare for a shot at goal.

SUPERSKILLS

❝ The overhead kick is spectacular but it's also a great weapon for a striker to possess. If ever I was manager of a football team I'd get my strikers to learn how to do a back somersault by encouraging them to learn gymnastics from an expert. If you know how to take off and how to land you can soon learn how to time the actual kick ❞

Below left: A scissors kick needs precise timing. I launch into the flight by leaning away from the ball and pushing off with my right leg.

Below centre: As my right leg leaves the ground my striking foot meets the ball in line with my head.

Below right: The follow-through is restricted as I fall to the ground but the kick has been successfully carried out.

Going for goal sometimes means the attacker is not in an orthodox kicking position, and this is where agility comes into the game. To be able to make firm contact with the ball when both your feet are off the ground needs confidence, skill and a high degree of flexibility not just in your physical approach to the game but also in your thinking.

The basics are actually the same; it's just that for some of the more acrobatic kicks the action takes place from a horizontal position, sometimes even upside down.

The *scissors kick* is the first of the off-the-ground forms of ball contact I'll deal with.

The simplest scissor kick is one from an upright position which is nothing more than a jump from the ground with your non-striking leg, and contact made with the kicking foot while both feet are still in the air. This can mean that you meet the ball earlier than your opponents might anticipate, therefore giving you an advantage, and it can also offer you the chance of volleying, or shooting at goal, when to wait for a moment would mean that the ball had reached ground level.

Perhaps the form of scissors which is most commonly used is a kick from the horizontal position, when the kicker has to reach for the ball while falling towards the ground, making contact with his 'upper' leg as the non-striking leg prepares to cushion his contact with the ground.

The expression 'scissors' describes the leg action. The non-kicking leg is projected to an area

just in front of where contact will be made, and the kicking leg is momentarily in the area behind the falling ball. As contact is made the non-striking leg is being brought back slightly into line with the ball, and the kicking leg is moving through the strike and following through in a cutting move, like a pair of scissors.

Get the basics right first – then the tricks

I must emphasize that the type of superskills being covered in these pages follow the basic skills. Young players often try to copy the big-name players they've seen doing acrobatics on the field, but you must remember that those stars have learned the basics inside out before turning on the fancy stuff.

The *overhead kick* is a crowd pleaser. A forward with his back to goal sees the ball above him and does a back somersault, getting both feet into the air up where his head would be, and kicking the ball when he's upside down.

It's probably one of the most difficult kicks to carry out correctly and that's why you don't see too many players doing it. One of the main reasons is because a lot of players perhaps don't have the confidence to throw themselves upside down because they know of the risks involved. You can miss the ball, misdirect the kick, or hurt yourself as you fall, so there is plenty to put you off when going for the overhead.

The timing is so important in an overhead that if you don't get it right all you end up doing is throwing yourself at a ball and putting yourself out of the game for a moment or two while you get back on your feet.

Gerd Müller, Pelé and Denis Law were all brilliant at the overhead kick, and it's all due to a player's confidence as well as agility. I've always thought that if ever I was manager of a team I would try and get my strikers to do a little bit of acrobatics, perhaps train with a gymnastics expert for a while, to get the confidence to try the spectacular and see if they can perfect the overhead and horizontal kicks.

If you have the confidence to do a *back somersault* then it can improve your play around the penalty area, but you have to know how to take off, and how to land or you can hurt yourself badly.

For most players the acrobatic kicks are not that important, but the more weapons a striker has the better he will be. If he's likely to score goals from any body position then he's a danger to the opposition and an asset to his team.

But I have to come back to basics again even with the spectacular. While the overhead kick goes away from the principles of kicking a ball when both feet are on the ground the back somersault simply reverses things. The head has to be under, rather than over, and the knee of the kicking leg below the ball as the foot comes through. It's an upright kick in reverse, and the eye-on-the-ball rule is rigidly applied.

Small, agile players are usually the most acrobatic and it's men like Diego Maradona and Hugo Sanchez that you'll see trying to carry out complicated and spectacular kicks. I've seen tall defenders being forced to clear their lines with an overhead kick, however, and doing so in style.

Kicking the ball backwards over your head is fairly simple to practise. A high bouncing ball, or a ball that is coming towards you through the air, can be flicked over the shoulder without you having to leave the ground. The higher you raise your kicking leg to make contact the closer you're coming to an overhead somersault kick.

Now put yourself in the situation where you're in the penalty area; the ball is above your head and in front of you as your back is turned to the direction you want the ball to go. If you're a defender your objective is to get the ball upfield and away from trouble, but if you're attacking it could be a chance to score.

By dropping your body to the ground and lifting your legs to make contact you're in the position for the upside-down volley, the kick being completed before you hit the turf.

Practise with care

It's a good skill to practise, but when attempting any kick which means that you'll finish up hitting the floor you must start by finding a soft landing area. A beach is ideal, the soft sand offering you a cushion on which to learn how you will land, before attempting the spectacular on the training field.

Top: Back to goal, the overhead kick begins as I fall towards the target.

Above: The striking leg punches the ball as I prepare for landing. Both legs are off the ground and my arm is outstretched to cushion the fall.

DRIBBLING

❛ If you're 90 per cent sure that a trick will come off try to beat your opponent with it. But if you aren't sure remember that soccer is a team game and a well-placed pass to a colleague will beat the opposition every time. The crowd love to see a ball player take on and beat a man – but they're not so chuffed when the defender wins the ball ❜

1 A slalom of cones creates a perfect course for testing your ball control, but any obstacles will do.

2 The ball stays close to my feet as I change direction, pushing it into the space between the cones. Concentration is essential so keep your eyes on the ball at all times.

3 The slalom gives a player the opportunity to practise close control and learn to twist and turn at speed.

4 Changing direction means a transfer of weight from one side of the body to the other – remember always to keep your eyes on the ball and never let it get too far away from you.

Once you've mastered simple techniques like passing the ball with the inside and outside of the foot you're well on the way to a skill which is very much a part of the game – the dribble.

The dribble is exactly what it sounds like; a weaving run with the ball under control meandering through opponents in the way that a stream would dribble its way around rocks.

You need to be able to play the ball confidently with both feet, and with all the contact surfaces of the foot.

The simplest way of practising and developing your skill to run with the ball and weave through obstacles is to place cones, or bricks, or even old cardboard boxes in a pattern a bit like a slalom course for a skier and to run between them and around them with the ball. Run to one end, turn and run back, weaving in and out of the obstacles, not letting the ball get away from your feet and not hitting the obstacles with either ball or feet.

Once you've mastered this type of control you can speed it up, running more quickly through the course.

What you're doing is running with the ball under control. You know where the ball is going and you have to position yourself to be able to play it with the next foot before it rolls out of your control. Never let it get too far away and never have it too close; you'll quickly find the correct position to be in full command.

The dribble is the ball player's way of keeping the ball in his possession. He's using his skills to

---

ROBSON'S TIPS

● *Learn close control by running with the ball through a series of obstacles, keeping the ball at your feet and not letting it hit any of the markers. Quicken your pace as you get better until you can sprint through.*

● *Remember that to beat your man you must have the situation under your control. You're waiting for him to commit himself, to go off balance and then you are through.*

● *Enlarge your repertoire of skills by watching the stars in action. Try to see how they trick an opponent and develop that skill as part of your game.*

● *The simplest way to beat an opponent is to push the ball past him and run. But remember that you're part of a team and someone may be backing you up.*

---

outwit an opponent and must be confident when attempting to dribble past a defender, because if he fails to beat him he gives possession to the other team and an attack breaks down.

Using your body

Not only does good foot control come into the dribble, but body positioning too. A shifting of

weight from one foot to the other can give an opponent the idea that you're going to change direction and if he moves to cover this could be the opportunity you've been waiting for and you can get past him by a quick return to the original side.

This is the basis of the *body swerve*, a dummy with your body which implies that you're going to run to the left, when in fact you have every intention of running to the right, and do so by switching your weight back at the moment when your opponent has taken the bait.

Fancy footwork will also throw a defender off the scent. Passing one foot over the ball, faking a pass, a shuffle of the feet to make him think you are changing direction, are all tricks which can be developed to improve your dribbling.

Study the stars

There's no better way of learning how to beat a man than by watching the way the top players do things. Try to emulate a ball-playing star who can play cat-and-mouse with a defender, showing him the ball, making him think that he has lost control, then at the correct moment racing past him with the opponent off-balance.

It's no use approaching a defender with a pre-conceived idea of the way you want to beat him, pushing the ball between his legs for the renowned 'nutmeg', or trying to make him 'buy' your 'dummy', or stepping over the ball to change direction. What you're waiting for is the moment when he has lost balance but you have still got the ball under control – then you're past him.

I don't think it's possible to describe just how you should go about beating your man, for dribbling is an individual skill which you must work on to gain confidence and increase ability. If you discover that you have a flair for this part of the game then you must develop it and build up a repertoire – but always remember that teams win matches and a well-timed pass to a colleague in a good position is another way through.

Above: The ball under close control, I transfer weight to my left foot as I swerve past an opponent.

4

TAKING CONTROL

❝ Don't make your leg a brick wall as the ball comes to you. Treat it as a follow-through in reverse, going back along the line of flight and taking the sting out of the ball so that it's under your control ❞

There's one skill which must come a close second in soccer's league table to kicking a ball, and that's the ability to take control. If a player can't control the ball he'll find himself with all sorts of problems, and the quicker he learns how to kill the flight, stop the bounce, and get the ball under his command the sooner he becomes a more complete soccer player.

The moment that the ball comes under the control of a player it's his to do with as he wishes; if the ball is not under control it won't go where the player wants it to, and that's the last thing he wants.

Imagine a high clearance coming towards you. The ball has travelled half the length of the field and is dropping to the ground. What happens next?

Well, let's look at it two ways. First, let's say that the player going to collect the ball has no idea of control, has never seen what happens to a football when it arrives under such circumstances. He looks at the ball, watches its flight and, as it lands, sticks out a tentative foot. The ball ignores him, bouncing two or three feet in front of him over his outstretched leg.

That may sound a little far-fetched, but we've all seen someone trying to trap a ball and being completely baffled when it has bounced away from him.

Our second situation sees a player under the same circumstances moving into the flight of the ball, positioning his body so that he is in line, and killing the ball as it reaches the ground by 'riding' its flight with his foot in the same way that someone catching a ball allows his hands to move backwards with it.

Just as the catcher would find it painful if he simply stuck a rigid hand in the path of the ball, the soccer player has to cushion the ball as it lands when making a successful trap.

There are times when it seems that the ball has a mind of its own; if a player lacks the skill to control it the ball will evade him. The player with control is master! Control is important – quick control essential.

Learning to 'kill' the ball

Killing the ball and getting it under your control can be done in a variety of ways. It's an easy skill to practise and is a development of the passing moves I described earlier. To learn basic control try a sidefoot pass onto a flat wall and as the ball rebounds take control with one movement and then kick the ball forward again.

By increasing the power of the original kick you'll find that the ball comes to you either much faster or from a different angle, and this gives you the chance to kill its flight by allowing it to follow the backward movement of your leg, toes turned outwards, until its movement is stopped between the inside of your foot and the ground.

Another simple way of killing the flight is to trap the ball between the sole of your foot and the ground, leaving your heel at just below the height of the ball, your toes slightly higher and using your foot as a wedge.

During play you rarely have time to ponder about which way you will kill the flight: you have to make up your mind as you get to the ball.

A favourite with my old pal Arnie Muhren was to catch the ball on the outside of his foot while the ball was above knee height. He would turn side-on to the approach, and ride the ball down its last few inches until the speed had gone out of it. The movement of his foot would send it forward and he would have it under his command.

Bottoms down!

You can trap the ball with the side of your calf, just above your ankle and below the knee, letting the leg move with the flight across your standing leg and into the angle between leg and ground which creates the 'trap'. Some players like to take control by catching the ball on the top of the boot and riding it to ground level, and I've even seen the rear end being used to good effect!

In my West Brom days Willie Johnston had a favourite trick that delighted the crowd. He would trap the ball by sticking out his seat as the ball came to earth and stun its bounce with a little upward movement as it struck his body. The ball would drop behind him, a quick turn and he was away!

I can't stress how important it is that you learn to take control of the ball quickly and efficiently. You can waste a lot of time, energy and advantage chasing after the ball if you haven't been able to trap it and place it under your command.

The ways that you can kill the ball are too numerous to attempt to list, but confident foot control is certainly a skill no soccer player can be without.

Right: The outside of the foot is a useful area for killing a ball. The raised leg projects the ball slightly forward of the receiver but well under his control.

Below left: A ball arriving from my right is caught on the inside of the foot – timing the flight is essential. Eyes remain on the ball at all times.

Below right: After cushioning the ball it is brought under control with a downward movement of the leg.

USING YOUR BODY

❝ Your body is just as important as your feet. It's a point that a lot of would-be soccer players forget, and they restrict their area of skill. Using your body to control the ball is a basic part of the game, and being able to play the ball off your chest and thighs is something that every young player should work at ❞

A soccer player can use any part of his body to control the ball with the exception of his hands and arms – unless he's a goalkeeper of course – and one of the most effective areas for control is the chest.

Because it's a fairly flat surface the chest allows you to cushion the ball without fear of it shooting off at an angle, and it acts as the perfect landing zone for a high ball that you don't want to head forward, and which you want to collect before it reaches ground level.

The ball is coming to you from a long kick downfield. You can see that you can get it under control and have the space around you to do so by using your chest. The method I use is fairly straightforward and one which anyone can try.

As the ball arrives I make sure that my elbows are sticking out, which widens the shoulders and gives me good balance. Just at the moment of impact – my eyes on the ball, chin above it – I drop my chest in a backward and downward movement, letting the ball 'rest' for a split second. My back is arched slightly and the ball has been caught; it drops to my feet and is under control.

It's quite an easy skill to practise. Simply lob a ball against a wall so that it comes back at the correct height and bring it under control in the way I've just described.

While the chest is the most obvious area of control other than the feet and head, you should also be aware of other parts of the body that can be used.

The thigh is ideal for stunning the ball. The inside will absorb its speed, the top will act as a cushion as it drops, and the outside can block its path and give you control. What you must be aware of is that a firmly hit ball can give you a nasty shock if it hits the inside or outside of your thigh and you haven't got yourself into position and prepared for its arrival.

Apart from the sting – which can warm you up on a cold day – you can be knocked off balance when using your thigh because to do so usually means that you are standing on one leg with the receiving leg held out at an angle, bent at the knee.

Passing with the body

The body can of course add to your armoury. The chest is not simply an area for catching the ball; it can also be used to project a pass to a colleague, and even score a goal.

The action is the reverse of that used for taking control. Instead of arching the shoulder forward and forming a concave shape with chest, arms and shoulders, the elbows go back, the chest is expanded and the ball bounces off it.

The same rule applies to the thighs. A backward movement will cushion the flight but if the ball is met with a limb which is moving in the opposite direction it will react in the same way as if it was being struck by a kicking action.

There are times in a game when it isn't possible to wait for the ball to drop to kicking height, when

Right: A high ball drops towards my chest. To kill its flight I cushion its landing with a slight backward movement of my body. Good balance and a wide stance make this possible.

Far right: As the ball is 'caught' my knees have pushed forward and my weight is now being supported by my toes.

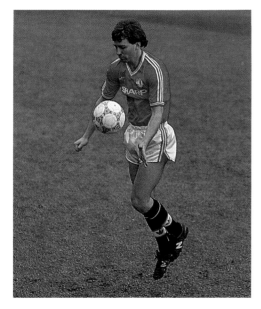

Far left: The ball drops under control and a straightening movement of my legs pushes my body forward.

Left: The right foot has reached the ground first and the ball is under my control.

Below: Controlling the ball on the thigh. The flight is killed by a catching movement, the body leaning back slightly for balance. Correctly controlled, the ball should drop just in front of you.

a blow with the thigh will do the trick. It could be a goal-line clearance, or a scoring attempt, and it's always worth a try.

Your body is part of your game and if you can produce the goods with feet, head, thighs and chest, you are well on the way to being an accomplished player.

ROBSON'S TIPS

● *When taking the ball on your chest follow the flight and ride the moment of impact by pushing back your elbows and bending your back. The ball will drop towards your feet.*

● *Expand your chest on impact and the ball will be projected forward. Remember that this is a good way of laying off a pass to a colleague when an opponent is expecting you either to head the ball or bring it down to your feet.*

● *The thigh punt – lobbing the ball forward by making contact just above the knee – can get you out of trouble if you haven't got time to get your foot to the ball. Kneeing it firmly will lift the ball over an opponent.*

● *A downward movement of the thigh from a raised knee position will help you take control. Ride the speed of the flight and bend your body forward as the leg is lowered; this helps you keep your balance and smother the ball.*

USING YOUR HEAD

❝ Being able to head the ball confidently under any circumstances is another step towards being a more complete soccer player. There are some players who have made it to the top without being good with their heads, but nowadays the cry is for more all-round ability, and that makes heading very important ❞

There are two golden rules to heading; they are simple but tremendously important. Rule one is never close your eyes. If you do, then you can't see where the ball is! Rule two is that the forehead is the one and only area with which you should try to head the ball.

Just as most beginners will try to kick a soccer ball with their toes, then many people make the mistake of trying to head the ball with the very top of their head. Not only does this hurt, but it also takes away any possibility of you having control over direction or distance.

So let's start at the beginning. You must watch the ball all the time. Throw the ball up against a wall and as it comes down let it bounce off your forehead. That's the basic principle of heading, because the flat, strong area above your eyes is perfect for projecting the ball forward.

To begin with, heading technique should be developed by learning to head the ball into an area on a wall which will return it to you at the correct height for repetition of the exercise. You'll soon discover that a slight projection of the neck will push the head at the ball and will increase the power on impact.

Forcing the head forward is the way that we gain distance in heading a ball, while turning the head so that contact is made at an angle to the flight gives us the opportunity to change the ball's direction.

When we head the ball we're using the same principles as volleying with our feet. We have to watch the flight, intercept the ball at the precise moment, and make good contact.

How to avoid a headache

For a small boy, heading the ball can seem a fairly frightening experience. A light plastic ball can give a totally false idea of what it's like to make contact with a leather soccer ball and that's why it's important to learn to do things properly.

I can't remember *not* heading the ball. I just did what the rest of my pals did and practised heading in the same way as I developed my kicking abilities. But there's every possibility that the first time I headed a soccer ball I simply stuck my head in the path of the ball and found out the hard way!

Pain can be a great teacher . . . but if you know the correct way then there's nothing to fear, and no need to suffer!

I don't want to give the impression that heading a soccer ball is going to cause you serious injury, but at the same time if you put your head in the way of a fierce drive then you'll realize that there's more to heading than most other areas of the game.

It's a good idea to get the feel of heading the ball by simply throwing a soccer ball into the air two or three feet above you and then letting it bounce off your forehead, watching it all the time and keeping those eyes open right up to the moment of contact.

You'll quickly find that it doesn't hurt, but you'll also see that simply letting the ball bounce off you isn't enough.

The head is part of the soccer player's armoury and for some players it's proved to be as vital as their shooting boots. So there's more to heading than using your forehead as a surface for the ball to bounce from. The head has got to be forced into the ball, with the neck muscles, shoulders and upper body all playing their part, and in some cases the whole body being used to add more power to head and ball contact.

Getting more power

Having built up confidence by basic heading practice, repetitive headers onto a wall, or lob-heading from partner to partner over a short distance, you've got to look to the next stage – going for more length.

Pick a target say ten yards in front of you, and throw the ball above your head in a tennis-serve style. Now if you just let the ball bounce off you it won't get anywhere near the target, so in order to lengthen the distance you have to use your body to force your head into the ball.

I do this by bending back from the waist, pushing my knees forward and slightly outwards, raising my hands in front of my chest and pushing my elbows out. My head goes back, but I keep my eyes on the ball and my head upright so that my forehead will make good contact. Just before impact my shoulders come up, my neck muscles begin to pull and I'm ready to head the ball.

What's happened is that I've wound my body into a spring, and at the moment of impact I'm going to let this spring unwind.

The first thing that happens is that the forehead makes contact with the ball, the neck pushes the head forward into it, and as the ball changes direction under my control the rest of the body follows through. The back, which has bent backwards, now goes forward, the shoulders and chest push towards the ball, and the arms and elbows come inwards after being spread out to the side.

If you imagine that you had a plank of wood standing upright with its base firmly anchored, and you had bent the wood over so that it would recoil when you released it, that's the sort of action you should try to get from your body.

By holding the head firmly in the contact position you're able to direct the ball forward. Your neck muscles and arms give you the strength to punch through and this is the secret of heading the ball any distance.

It's essential to follow through the action when kicking, and the same rule applies to heading, even though the follow-through may not seem as natural as with the feet. Because you are swinging your leg in an arc from the hip your foot can follow through naturally, but with the head it's the body which pushes into the ball to make the follow-through.

And as with the volley, if you allow the contact surface to lean back, and you let your head drop backwards at the point of contact a headed ball will go upwards. If the shoulders and head move backwards the ball will usually go into the air when the foot makes contact on a kick, and the same principle applies with the head. So if you're trying to keep the ball low the forehead should stay firm and push forward on the line you're aiming for.

Mastering the angles

I've given you a clue to a way of adding variety to your heading, and that's by moving the head 'off square'. If the head falls back as the ball arrives on the forehead then you can play a delicate header to a colleague, direct the ball over an opponent, or even back-head it over the defence just by a sort of reverse nodding action; but the ball still comes off the forehead!

Sometimes a player will make contact with the ball with the side of his head or the edge of his forehead, but even for angled heading the contact area stays the same.

ROBSON'S TIPS

● *Never close your eyes when heading the ball. Try to keep them open right through contact – or at least until the moment you feel the ball on your forehead.*

● *The top and the side of your head are 'no-go' heading areas, unless it's a real emergency. The forehead is the only area to use for heading, whether straight or angled. If you catch a firmly hit ball on the top of your head you'll be in for a shock!*

● *Push your forehead through the ball and use your neck muscles to keep your head in a firm position.*

● *Remember that it's just as important to follow through with your head as it is when kicking the ball.*

To change the direction of the ball you should twist the neck and shoulders and force the head onto the line that you're trying to achieve.

You must have seen players running towards a ball that's being crossed from the opposite side of the field, and then heading it at right angles to the line they're following. They do this by jumping into the path of the flight, pulling back their neck and head, then pushing the forehead through the ball in the direction of the target. The ball gets added power to its flight, changes direction and the player finishes his jump still travelling on the original line. It's a skill which needs plenty of practice, but an accomplished header of a soccer ball is another major asset to a team, no matter what position he plays.

Far left: Heading the ball correctly requires concentration. Eyes remain open to follow the flight, arms are raised as the head is pushed into the ball.

Left: When heading a ball off the ground the body acts as a spring to give greater power. Shoulders and head must push forward into the flight.

HEADING FOR GOAL

When you're scoring goals it doesn't matter how they go in the net as long as they go in. Obviously there are parts of your body that you can't use for scoring, although Maradona might not agree there! No, you just get to the ball and get it across the line any way you can – provided it's within the rules

Being able to score goals with your head is a technique every young player should work on, and not just strikers. It's important that you understand the principles of heading for goal and the simple rules you have to follow.

First, you must be able to judge the flight of the ball and pick the spot where you hope to intercept it with your head. Second, and perhaps more important, you must always know where the target is without spending too much time looking for it.

There are people in the game who earn the tag natural goal scorers. Ian Rush is perhaps the best example in the modern game, and Jimmy Greaves was one in the past – or so they tell me! They waste no time in the 'box'; if the ball is there they know just what they want to do with it, and always seem to know where the goal is.

Ian Rush is perhaps a better header of the ball than Jimmy Greaves was, but they both possess the same instinct of judging just where the target is and hitting it.

You have to develop this skill through practice especially when you're going for goal with your head, because you can't take your eye off the ball even for a second. The more you have developed this skill the more chance you have of scoring.

Timing is vital in most parts of the game, not least when you're heading. Usually when heading for goal you have to time your jump to beat a defender to the ball, and make contact with your forehead at the point which will give you the best angle on the goal.

A ball being played across the face of the goal needs to be met in the air at an angle which would take you somewhere beyond the far post if you carried on travelling. By running into the flight, and jumping to make contact, you can head the ball downwards by pushing hard with the neck, or make a looping header by keeping the head fairly upright as you reach the ball.

The diving header

There are times when you can't reach a cross with an outstretched leg, but a diving header will do the trick. This skill needs to be practised hard for perfection, but can be very effective.

Imagine a low cross coming into the six-yard area from the right. You're running towards it and know that the ball will pass the point of contact several feet in front of you. The only way to get to it is the dive, so you throw yourself full length, arms in front of you but below the height of your body. You have to keep watching the ball and aim to make contact only with your forehead.

What happens when you connect is that the ball is projected towards goal with tremendous force because it has the full momentum of your body behind it, and provided you're on target there's every chance that you'll score.

It's a lot easier to dive into a ball than to try to make contact with your foot in the circumstances I've just described. But remember that you must know how to land correctly, and that there is a high risk involved in this type of move, because defenders may well be trying to volley clear.

Right: When heading for goal you must time your jump so you're above the ball at the point of contact.

Centre right: Strike by pushing your forehead into the ball, keeping your eyes open all the time.

Far right: By directing the ball downwards you can create problems for a goalkeeper who will have to dive to make a save and might be beaten by the bounce as well as the power of the header.

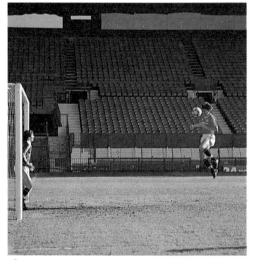

ROBSON'S TIPS

● Timing your run and jump is essential. Aim to meet the ball at the point where you can make best contact.

● Always try to get above the ball, since this increases the number of ways you can head for goal.

● If your back is to goal try a back-flick, tossing the ball off your forehead. Move your head as if you were flicking back your hair and the ball will loop up behind you.

Above: Here I am in action for Manchester United against Arsenal at Highbury.

HEADING IN DEFENCE

Rather than just jumping and heading anywhere try to pick out a spot where you're able to use the ball to your advantage. Sometimes a defender's only option is to head away from goal, but often he can pass to a colleague. You have to try to use your head in more ways than one

The aim of most defenders when making contact with the ball in their penalty area is to get it upfield as far and wide as they can. This is why heading for distance is an essential skill for any defender.

Taller players usually make the best defenders and are able to use their height to get above their opponents to win the ball. But agility and being able to judge the flight and time your jump at the ball are just as essential for a defender as an attacking player.

The object of the defensive header is reversed: instead of trying to head into the goal, the defender is looking for an area outside the penalty box where a colleague can pick up and take the ball away from danger.

Today's defenders are often faced with problems from corners where the attacking side has placed a man on the near post – that's the post closer to the corner the kick is being taken from – whose aim is to back-flick the ball across goal with his head.

The defender must be ready to intercept this type of cross by either getting to the ball before the attacking player, or timing his jump so that he's above the opponent at the moment of contact.

The golden rule: stay goal-side

The golden rule for any defender is not to let an opponent get across in front of him. If he does he's faced with all sorts of problems and his goal will be threatened.

Defenders have to make sure that when they go for a high ball they attack it with confidence.

Actually a defender has far more scope when it comes to heading away from goal than an attacker has in heading at the target. While the attacker must be accurate, the defender can aim for any area away from the penalty zone, or even out of play for a corner or a throw-in if he is under pressure.

So while an attacker will be hoping to make contact in an area close enough to goal for him to have a chance of scoring, the defender can aim to intercept the ball earlier and get it away from the danger zone.

Being able to jump to a reasonable height and at the same time watch the flight of the ball and get your head to it make defensive heading a skill which must be practised to reach any sort of reasonable standard. It's no good just jumping a few inches as the ball passes over your head; you must be able to get yourself into the air and *attack* the ball.

If you allow an attacking player to get to the ball before you do he's going to create problems. Your aim is to beat him to it, and even if you fail to make contact with your jump you'll probably have done enough to prevent the man you're marking from getting a clear run and good contact.

You should also try to develop strength in the neck muscles and the shoulders. The more your heading skill grows the greater value it will be to you and your team-mates.

Frank Stapleton is the perfect example of a player who has developed his heading ability to a high standard. He's equally skilled either going for goal when in a striking position or heading away when he defends at corners. By being able to anticipate the movement of either a colleague or an opponent I've seen Frank not only score some great goals with his head but also save us from difficult situations.

Keep it simple

Another secret of the defensive header is to make it simple and effective. There's no time for you to try any clever tricks in defence: the aim is to get that ball as far away from your goal as possible.

Again the diving header can be put to good use, but this time we're trying to get the ball away from goal. Let's imagine the situation I described in the previous section. The ball is being crossed low across the face of the goal. The attacking player is hoping to intercept it at a point where his diving header will send the ball towards goal, and the defender obviously wants to do the opposite.

The odds are in favour of the defender, which is why you might see 20 crosses going into a penalty area during a game and very few goals. The attacker has that small target, but the defender will simply want to make contact with the ball and get it away.

By diving straight into the ball on the opposite 'flight path' the defender can head it back in the direction it came from, while by angling his head slightly as he meets the ball he can either send it left or right, for a corner or out of the penalty area towards the touchline.

There are times when a defender may have to use the back-flick to clear the ball, perhaps when he's under pressure on his own goal-line. Here he must be confident that he can head the ball over the bar, giving away a corner but preventing a goal.

On other occasions his header may be a last line of defence as he stands his ground on the goal-line and has to head the ball out with the goalkeeper beaten. This may be a fierce shot, and here he must have great confidence in his ability to do the correct thing.

I can remember being put in situations where if I failed to head the ball I would have more or less given a goal away. At times like that you have to know exactly what you're trying to do. Even though some headers look spectacular, it's usually a case of returning to basics: watch the flight, keep your eyes open and strike the ball firmly with your forehead.

It is often difficult to convince young players that they will make good defenders. The attraction of playing soccer for many is the thrill of beating an opponent and scoring a goal and at first it seems that there is little glamour attached to being centre-back.

However the emergence of players like Terry Butcher, and Kevin Ratcliffe who use their physical attributes as well as their skill, has made defending more of an art than it may have been in the past.

A tall strong youngster with speed and ability could find that he can get more satisfaction from his game playing in the defence than he would in a striker's role even though the headline stealers are usually the players up front. If he can offer his side a solid foundation on which to build he will

ROBSON'S TIPS

● When heading out of defence never let an opponent get across in front of you; always make his chance of getting to the ball more difficult than yours. Meet the ball early and away from the target area to give you more chance of clearing without risk.

● If a fiercely hit ball is coming at you and you want to head it clear, don't let the ball hit you – you must attack the ball. Keep your eyes open and push your forehead into the ball.

● Distance is the objective of most defensive headers, so practise heading for distance to improve your defending skills.

be of far more value than a player who might score a few goals during a season.

Of course there are many centre-backs who get their names on the scoresheet and that is where height and good use of the head can put them in an advantageous position.

Below left: A defensive header to clear danger. I time my jump to get above an attacker.

Below right: I meet the ball as my opponent approaches and head over him into space.

AERIAL COMBAT

' There's a lot of strength involved in aerial challenges, and this is something that a player must work on in training. Don't be afraid of the challenge; if your timing is good and you've learned how to jump high, let your opponents do all the worrying '

Below left: Beating an opponent to the ball is often a question of anticipation. Playing in defence I can follow the flight of a ball coming towards me better than an opponent who has his back to it.

Below centre: By timing my jump I can get to the ball first.

Below right: Defenders should always have the upper hand when it comes to clearing high balls played in their direction.

There's one major skill a player can develop without using a ball, and that's his ability to outjump an opponent in aerial combat. Winning the ball in the air is vitally important, especially in front of goal, and whether you're a defender or an attacker you need to be able to spring off the ground to gain the advantage over your marker.

I've spent hours practising a high jump, not in the style of someone taking part in an athletics competition – I don't think the Fosbury Flop would go down too well during a game of soccer – but in a way that helps me to get my head as high into the air as possible.

This is the first step towards success at aerial combat. Once you've mastered the skill of heading the ball from a standing position, and learned the basics of jumping into the flight, you've then got to introduce another aspect of the game – being able to hold off a challenge while getting your head to the ball.

Climbing to success

The arms and elbows are the secrets behind a good, strong, high challenge. You'll quickly find that you can 'climb' into the air by using the upper part of your body, rather than just jumping up with your arms by your sides.

You can actually gain extra height in aerial combat if an opponent jumps up under your elbow, because his added momentum will lift you that step further and perhaps win the ball for you.

However you must remember that the use of the arms and elbows to fend off an opponent is

illegal. You're using them to take you into the air and give you some protection, not as a weapon of attack.

When you jump at the ball with an opponent you're trying to get your head to it before he does, and the higher you can jump the better. If you know that you can leap two or three feet off the ground and if you add this to your actual height it gives you some sort of idea where your head should be at the point of contact. Even if your opponent may not be able to jump as high, and gives you the advantage of reaching the ball at an earlier point, he will still be able to challenge and put you under pressure.

Confidence and timing are two of the main

skills for good aerial combat: the confidence to jump early and get well off the ground, and the timing which instinctively tells you where you should be to meet the ball.

Strength also plays a major part, but this is all part of training for soccer. The all-round player has to build up his body strength and his ability to cope with an opponent jumping at him in a challenge for a high ball.

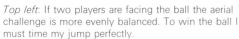

Top left: If two players are facing the ball the aerial challenge is more evenly balanced. To win the ball I must time my jump perfectly.
Above: I get above my opponent, holding off his efforts to get to the ball and head it clear.
Top right: In an attacking role I've got round a defender onto the side from which a cross is arriving. My jump into the flight is positive.
Centre right: Both of us are off the ground, the defender jumping towards the ball in the opposite direction from the flight, while I cross the flight path at a slight angle.
Bottom right: I can hold off the challenge and strike towards goal thanks to anticipation and timing.

THE TACKLE

' When the ball is out of your reach, but you know that you can get to it by throwing yourself into a slide tackle, that's the moment to use it. But don't make every tackle a slide tackle because you can easily be put out of the play by a clever opponent. If he knows you're going to slide, he'll move the ball away from you at the last moment and you'll be on the ground as he goes past you ,

Being able to tackle an opponent with confidence and win the ball when under pressure is not simply a way of adding a vital dimension to your game: it's probably one of the most satisfying parts of playing soccer.

The basic rule of making a good tackle is to use the whole of your body weight. Don't just let your leg hang in front of the person you're challenging or he will brush you aside. You need determination and strength, and most of all the will to win the ball.

What you're attempting to do is to put your foot behind the ball and block its movement from the person who's playing it. You're challenging for possession and any challenge has to be wholehearted or it's just a waste of time.

It's vitally important that for an upright challenge you get your body above the ball as your foot makes contact, or you will risk injury. A limp outstretched leg has no strength; you will be off balance and easily beaten.

So when making the challenge watch your opponent and wait for the right moment to attack. He'll be trying to beat you, but provided that you

can jockey him into a position where you feel you have the advantage then you can attack.

There's nothing to fear in making a tackle, even against an opponent who is bigger than you are, provided you follow the basic rules. You have as good a chance of coming away with the ball as your opponent has of keeping it under his control.

Timing the challenge

That's where timing the challenge tips the scales in the tackler's favour. The man in possession is waiting for you to make your move so that he can beat you, but if you hold off long enough he will be forced to try to get away from you. That's the moment you're waiting for: keeping your weight above the challenging leg, you strike for the ball.

Don't lean back but put your weight forward on the leg which is going at the ball, and the tackle is made. Provided that you haven't held back you'll have forced the ball away from your opponent's control and perhaps even made him lose his balance, giving you freedom to play on.

Size should not really come into it. I often have to challenge men much taller than me, and there

Right: I wait for the moment when an opponent is off balance before making the tackle.

Centre right: I push the ball away from the attacker and onto a line I want to follow. My opponent is still off balance and has to regain his feet before turning.

Far right: The ball is pushed free, the attacker is beaten and I'm clear to run upfield.

are times when smaller players will challenge me successfully. Tackling involves balance, timing, strength and confidence – and if all these things are put together they'll make a successful challenge.

The straightforward upright tackle from the front is a trial of strength and skill between challenging players, but there are other ways of making sure of winning the ball from an opponent.

The slide tackle

If you're chasing the man in possession you can always intercept the ball if he pushes it too far in front of him, provided you have the speed to make the challenge.

At the same time if you can run across his path you may be able to slide tackle and win the ball, but this type of challenge should be used only if you are positive that you will get to the ball. There's nothing worse than feeling yourself sliding past an opponent, unable to get back to your feet, while he steps on the ball and makes you look foolish, or heads towards your goal.

When you go to make a slide tackle remember two things: you're committing yourself to the challenge and must not fail; and, throughout the movement, you have to keep your eye on the ball, not the player's feet.

The slide tackle can be executed in a variety of ways; some players prefer to go down onto the outside of their thigh, and travel towards the ball in the same direction as the man who is running with it. Peter Beardsley is a fine exponent of this

type of challenge. He'll race alongside his opponent then, timing his challenge correctly, he'll go down on his left thigh and as he's sliding along the ground he'll play the ball away from the opposition by swinging his right leg across his body.

The more orthodox slide tackle is to run at your opponent either from the front or the side, and go down on the knee and calf of the non-tackling leg, supporting your body with this leg as the other makes contact with the ball.

With this type of tackle the end result, apart from winning the ball, is that you are going to finish up on the ground and out of the action for a moment. That's why it's essential that you know exactly what you're doing before sliding in.

You must learn to take a tumble in a game, and the slide tackle is one of the simplest ways of picking up the technique of falling properly. When you tackle with your right foot, your right arm and elbow should be ready to support your landing. If you use the left foot the opposite applies.

Don't hold back

Perhaps I should also stress that there's less likelihood of you getting hurt if you give 100 per cent in the tackle. If you hold back at all you are risking injury.

When making a tackle a player can genuinely mistime his challenge and make contact with the opponent rather than the ball. This is a foul of course, but one way of making sure that your tackle is fair is always to watch the ball. If you take your eyes off the ball things can go wrong.

BALL WINNING

' You must be in the right place at the right time to win the ball. You have to learn to read the game so that when you see a situation developing you can anticipate the next move and intercept the ball before it reaches its target. Quick thinking can mean as much in soccer as being quick on your feet, and a combination of both is something most top players have '

There are other ways of winning the ball apart from actually taking it off an opponent in a tackle, and in this section I'd like to give you a few examples of when ball-winning should come into your game, and how to use speed and quick thinking to take advantage of the opposition.

I mention speed first of all because if you are able to run faster than an opponent there's every chance that you'll be able to get the better of him in certain areas of the game.

If the slower player breaks away with the ball under his control, by running alongside him you can 'nick' it from him. This 'steal' is seen in a game of soccer almost as many times as an actual tackle, and you do it simply by flicking the ball away from the opponent while on the run.

It isn't a slide tackle, but it can have the same result, because there's every chance that you'll lose balance if you're running at anything but a fairly slow pace and finish up on the ground. So, just as with the slide tackle, the 'steal' must be carried out only when you're 100 per cent sure that you're going to get the ball – not simply trip your opponent and give away a free kick.

I think that there are risks with this type of move, and I much prefer the straightforward tackle. Because you're not putting your full body weight behind your challenge there's also a chance that you could get hurt, as well as failing to win the ball.

Winning the ball is actually another aspect of being able to read the game. Nobody can teach you to read a game of soccer; it's something

which comes through practice, and the experience of what happens when a player is put in a certain type of situation.

You know that if a winger has the ball and likes to run down the outside, you must make sure that

1 I challenge an opponent, forcing him to run wide before making a tackle.

2 Because he is close to the touchline the attacker hesitates to turn inside. This gives me the opportunity to strike, snatching the ball away from my opponent's possession.

3 A body movement to the right gives me correct balance with my weight momentarily on my left side.

4 With the ball under my control I can move upfield as the opponent has to turn to chase.

1

2

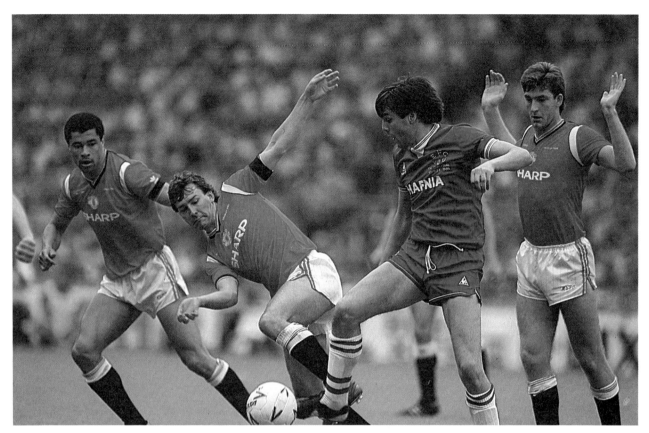

he can't by positioning yourself so that he feels impeded. If an opponent is renowned for using his left foot, make sure that the ball is pushed to his right side by covering the left.

'Closing down' space

I could go on forever giving examples of what you look for when trying to win the ball, but there are some things you should always remember. When a man in under pressure he's probably going to play the ball into space so that a team-mate can help him out; so you have to 'close down' that space in order to win the ball. If he 'telegraphs' a pass – in other words makes it so obvious that he's going to play the ball to a colleague – and you can get there first, that's the time to make your challenge.

Interception is a great skill to develop, and quick thinking to read a situation can pay off. Try to anticipate the next move and put yourself into a challenging position, but don't commit yourself until you feel that the moment is right.

I battle for the ball against Graeme Sharp of Everton during the 1985 Football Association Cup final.

3

4

TAKING GOALKICKS

' A keeper's long kicking can be a great advantage to his side. Most teams try to get the ball into their keeper's hands from a goalkick because this gives him better control and greater distance, but it's up to the opposition to stop this sort of move. Pressure on the players around the box forces him to take a long kick from a dead ball '

The goalkick is the kick from the edge of the six-yard box which restarts play after the ball has crossed the goal-line, providing it was last touched by a player from the opposing side. The principle of taking such a kick is simple: the goalkeeper has to get the ball down the field and try to find a team-mate.

But of course there's far more to it than that. The goalkeeper is driving a dead ball and must put all his effort into such a kick, but without losing any control. He must practise this part of his game to get length and accuracy with his kicking and try to perfect a style which brings him a high percentage of success.

He shouldn't use his toes or the side of the foot to kick the ball. He should get his foot under the ball and power it upfield with the top of his foot.

Today's top teams have developed tactics which even include goalkicking, with full-backs moving wide to draw an opposing forward with them and leave space for the keeper to play the ball short out of the box to the centre-backs. Or the reverse can happen, leaving the full-back free.

A lot of sides don't bother to cover the defence at a goalkick. They simply try to win back the ball after the keeper has been allowed to play it upfield.

Failure rate
It's obvious that a goalkeeper prefers to play the ball upfield from his hands, using the volley or half-volley to give him greater distance and improved accuracy, and that's the thinking behind the short goalkick.

The tactics used by the majority of top English sides is to send the forwards in at the full-backs to stop the keeper sending a short kick to them, and so forcing him to take the long 'dead ball' kick off the ground. The failure rate on this type of kick is quite high, and in any game it's possible that a goalkeeper might make a mistake from a goalkick.

Outfield players have also got to be prepared for goalkicking because under certain circumstances they might be called on to take the kick. Of course they can't play the ball short to the full-back and pick up the return (unless they have actually replaced the keeper in goal), so they will usually opt for distance.

It's quite a common sight to see defenders in teams from mainland Europe taking goalkicks, and while keepers should practise their dead-ball kicking there's no reason why – if the player is good between the posts – his kicks shouldn't be taken by a defender.

The 'short' kick
It is possible for a short goalkick to be taken by a full-back or outfield player and still be played upfield via the keeper's clearance kick. But to do this the goalkeeper must make a run out of the penalty area as the goalkick is taken by his

The goalkick is a long strike upfield. Body weight is supported by the non-striking leg which is alongside the ball at the moment of contact; outstretched arms give good balance and the head stays above the ball.

●*If you have to take a goalkick you must use a long enough run to build up speed at the moment of contact and keep your head down as you strike through the ball – as for any long pass.*

●*The short goalkick allows the keeper to pick up the ball from the return. But defenders must be aware of the keeper's intentions and ready to play back to him from the short kick.*

●*The defending side has the advantage when a long goalkick is played upfield beyond the halfway line. But the shorter kick, perhaps to an unmarked man in a wide position, helps keep possession.*

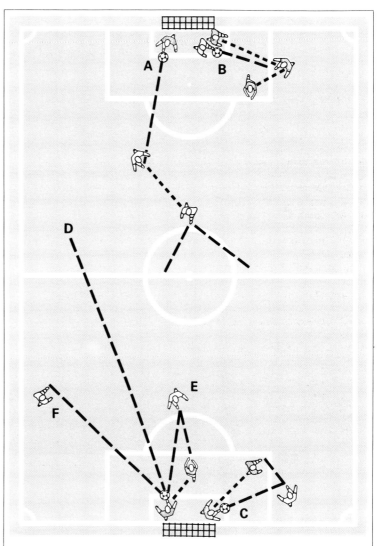

colleague, playing the ball back into the box with his feet before picking it up. Remember that the opposition will be on the lookout for this ploy and will put pressure on the defence to prevent the tactic being used.

The role of the defender at the goalkick is to cover parts of the field where the ball might fall if the keeper miscues it, or to make sure that the opposing front men don't get into a position where they can prevent a back pass if that move is being used. But for the attacking side a goalkick can be used to good advantage.

If a full-back is slow to control a short goalkick, the attacking side must try to get a man into the penalty area between the full-back and the goalkeeper to stop the outfield player from returning the ball.

Extra pressure by another attacker can force the full-back into making an error, and it's important that attackers are quick to read a situation that can give them the advantage. Defenders, of course, should be ready to support a colleague in trouble.

Using your options

If the goalkick has been taken successfully and the ball played well upfield the attacking players of the side which has taken the kick will be trying to keep possession and use the move to their advantage. But because they'll have their backs to the goal they're attacking they are at a disadvantage when receiving the ball. That's why it's important to get the ball to a player in an open position from this type of situation, and why defences will try to give their keeper the option of kicking or throwing the ball out by returning a goalkick to him.

The defender in the side *facing* the goalkick is trying to position himself so that he can get over the top of the attacker and head the ball back downfield as far as possible.

Here again he has the advantage because he's facing 'the right way' as the ball arrives and

Goalkick variations: **A** The keeper plays the ball to a back-four player who is just outside the penalty area. He can run forward and pass to a colleague in any direction. **B** The keeper runs from the penalty area and the goalkick is taken by a colleague. He kicks the ball to the edge of the box, the keeper dribbles the ball back into the penalty area, then picks it up to clear. (This method can be used only when the opposition players are well away from the penalty area.) **C** The ball is played to an unmarked full-back on the edge of the penalty area.

The keeper then runs forward to the front edge of the box and picks up the return pass to clear downfield. **D** The goalkick is directed to the wide midfield player on the left. A kick from the opposite side of the box can be used for bringing the wide right-sided player into the play. **E** A short goalkick is returned to the keeper by a back-four player. **F** A short angled goalkick to an unmarked defender who can then carry the ball forward down the flank.
■■ ■■ Path of ball
■ ■ ■ ■ Path of player

doesn't need to turn as his opponent does.

Young players should remember that they may not have the strength to kick a dead ball great distances, so it's essential for them to learn both how to drive the ball over the heads of players close to the penalty area and how to play the short goalkick well and safely.

FREE KICKS

❛ If you watch soccer games you'll soon realize how many different ideas can be used with a free kick. Don't be afraid to experiment – the element of surprise is something which every good team should have ❜

The free kick gives you the opportunity to play the ball once without being challenged. With a direct free kick you can of course have a shot at goal, but nine times out of ten the free kick has simply given you possession and it's up to your team to make the best use of it.

For the defence the free kick against you can sometimes be used to your advantage. You have time to mark up players who could have been free a moment or two earlier, and it gives you the chance to win back the ball.

As for the attack, they must always try to use any free kick in their opponent's half of the field as a method of getting a scoring chance at the target.

A long ball played into the penalty area could

Top right: The defence has formed a three-man wall. I can either try to bend a shot around the blockade or pass to a colleague.

Centre right: I opt for the chipped pass to my striker, playing the ball above the wall to the right.

Bottom right: My team-mate runs in to strike at goal as the defenders turn to cover.

set up a scoring opportunity, or a short pass to a colleague running at the ball can be a surprise tactic to employ as you try to find a way through the defensive cover.

The defence's role for a free kick in their own half of the field is to get everybody back 'behind the ball', and to cover all the spaces where an opponent might be able to make a run.

If the opposition has tall players in their side with good aerial power you must put your own tall players up against them. Players who are shorter and perhaps quick at anticipating where the ball is going to be played next should be in a position where they can intercept a knock-down header from the tall men.

Once again the defender's aim must be to stop a forward from getting across in front of him because it can prevent him seeing the ball and making contact with it. The rule applies in reverse for the attacker, who doesn't want the defender

to beat him to the ball and rob him of a scoring chance or the opportunity to add to the move.

Touch-and-shot

When I'm taking a free kick on the outside of the opposition's penalty area I'm looking for a *touch-and-shot*: tipping the ball to a colleague who can have a go at goal, or having a shot myself. If you have a free kick in that position you have to get a shot in or the move is wasted.

You can use a variety of tactics at a free kick: a short pass then a backheel to a team-mate who's coming in from an unexpected angle; a runner going round behind the defence to get on the end of a chip; a bending shot from a direct kick.

But whatever ideas you employ to create a scoring opportunity it's important that your team-mates understand exactly what you're trying to achieve. Free kick tactics have to be worked out in advance or the chance will be wasted.

A quickly-taken free kick can often cause problems for the opposition. Here I'm pushing a short pass to a team-mate before the opposing team has time to organize its cover.

TAKING THROW-INS

❝ For some reason players get into the habit of bouncing the ball so that it comes up to a team-mate's stomach. It's the easiest way I suppose, just dropping the ball in front of a colleague, but you put him in all kinds of trouble. He can't control a rising ball quickly and before he knows where he is a defender is hooking his legs around him to knock the ball away. Throw directly to feet or chest to give your team-mate a real chance ❞

The technique used in throwing a ball back into play after it has gone into touch is fairly straightforward, and most young players know the rules. Both feet must be behind the line when the throw is taken, and neither foot must leave the ground. The ball has to be brought back behind the head, held in both hands and thrown into play in a movement that projects the ball forward with the arms kept straight.

Simple enough? Yes, but there's more to taking a throw-in than that.

When you take a throw-in remember that the idea is for your side to keep possession. You've been given the advantage because the opposition have been last to play the ball when it went over the touchline. It's no use throwing the ball where an opponent can intercept, or to one of your colleagues who is either well-marked or in a position where he will have difficulty gaining control. You must *think* before you throw.

The same rule applies to those hoping to receive the ball from the throw. It's no use standing around – you've got to move into position, create space by trying to lose your marker and get ready to collect the ball.

The thrower has to get the ball to a colleague in a way that he can control it. I often get annoyed, even with players at top level, who throw the ball to me so that it bounces just in front of me and up towards my stomach.

That's no good at all. You should be able to take the ball under immediate control, or knock it off to a team-mate straight away.

Throws must go straight to your feet, drop on your thigh or your chest, or be at a height where you can get your head to the ball comfortably.

Using the long throw
Some players are able to throw the ball such a distance that a throw-in becomes as useful as a corner, and teams can use the same tactics in this situation as they would if the ball was being kicked into the penalty area.

Long throwers have built up power in their arms and back but they are not necessarily the

A quick throw creates an opening for Manchester United. I rarely take throws but here, against Everton at Old Trafford, I saw the opportunity of a breakthrough and quickly got the ball back in play.

1 Losing your marker is necessary to gain advantage at a throw-in. Dummy runs, twists and changes of direction can put an opponent off balance.

2 The ball is on its way, I've created space and I'm anticipating where the throw will land.

3 I keep my eyes on the ball accelerating away from the opposition.

4 Because the ball arrives at my feet I can take immediate control. A ball which bounces just in front of a receiver is a disadvantage.

tallest or even strongest players. It's a good attacking move if you have a player like this in your side, because he can drop a ball on the near post for a team-mate to flick on, just as he would for a corner.

It always looks good if a player can manage to produce a good long throw, but young players must master the basics of an orthodox throw-in before going for distance. Long throwers should always remember that if the opposition has marked up all the players in positions where the long ball would drop, then they should be thinking ahead and ready to play a short throw to a better placed man.

When the opposition is taking a throw you must always be trying to read the situation so that you can intercept. This isn't as hard as it sounds because the ball isn't travelling as hard from a throw-in as it would be from a pass. No-one can throw the ball in as strongly as it could be kicked and the chances of you getting to it first are fairly high.

TAKING PENALTIES

❝ The perfect penalty is the shot which is hit powerfully at the best target area, just behind the post in the side netting. It should have enough swerve on the ball to curl it away from the keeper's hands, even if he dives the right way. But goalkeepers are getting more agile and better at stopping penalties. If they go the right way nowadays there's a good chance that they'll at least get a hand to the ball ❞

There are a lot of theories about how a penalty should be taken, but I reckon there's really only one way – and that's the simplest. You pick the corner of the goal you intend to aim for, and kick the ball as firmly and as accurately at that area as you can. It sounds simple and it is; provided that you do everything correctly, there's nothing the goalkeeper can do to stop the ball, even if he guesses right.

If you're taking a penalty you should place the ball on the spot so that it's 'sitting' well. Don't put it in a rut or a patch of mud, and make sure that *you* place the ball, no-one else. In some amateur games I've seen an angry goalkeeper slam the ball onto the spot and retreat to his line still protesting about the penalty being awarded and the poor kicker has almost broken his foot because the crafty keeper has made sure the ball is stuck fast!

So place it well, and approach the ball in the same way that you would if you were going to drive a pass. Forget there is a goalkeeper: let *him* worry about *you* – you're the one with the advantage. Pick your spot in one of the two corners and aim for it, trying to hit the ball into the side netting between the post and the stanchion.

The keeper will try to guess which way you're going to hit the ball and you should hit it firmly enough to prevent him from getting to it even if he moves the correct way.

Contrasting styles
There are many different styles used by penalty takers in the game and for contrast you can't

ROBSON'S TIPS

● *Take a run up long enough for you to feel confident that you'll strike the ball well, but short enough for you to have perfect timing with your shot.*

● *Don't change your mind. Decide where you're going to put the ball and go for it. Don't let the goalkeeper trick you into putting the ball into a part of the goal you don't want it to go to. You're the one with the advantage, so use it.*

really get further apart than two team-mates, Danish internationals Jan Molby and Jesper Olsen.

Jan takes a penalty the way that I think they should be taken; he runs up and puts the ball firmly in the spot he's picked, and he has a very high success rate. But just to show that different methods can be successful Jesper's system is totally the opposite, yet his record for club and country speaks for itself.

The Olsen style is to put a stutter in his approach, to change feet to unsettle the keeper. He will even wait until the goalkeeper has started to dive one way and stroke the ball the other. Impressive, but it needs ice-cool nerves.

When I take a penalty I don't really feel any

1

2

A successful penalty – Israel goalkeeper Avi Ran dives one way as I shoot to the other! A low powerful shot to the corner of the goal usually leads to success for the penalty taker.

pressure on me to score unless the game is at a vital point. If the penalty would give us the lead with a few minutes to go, obviously you feel differently than you would if you were 3-0 up. But the technique stays the same.

Youngsters should score

Young players, especially small boys playing in what to them are big goalmouths, should find it easier to score from a spot kick than does a top professional. The reason is simple – they don't have a 'full-size', top-level goalkeeper facing them!

If a tall top-level keeper decides to go the way you happen to be kicking the ball then he's got a very good chance of at least getting a hand to the shot. Goalkeepers have become very skilful and nowadays referees don't seem too keen to enforce the rule that says that their feet should not move until the kick is taken.

1 The approach for a penalty must be positive. Hesitation (unless deliberate) will give the keeper an advantage.

2 Contact is a firm strike with the instep, driving the ball towards the left-hand side of the target.

3 Even though the keeper has anticipated the direction of the shot its power and flight take it beyond his reach.

4 The punch-like shot requires a short follow-through but the kicker must always follow the flight of the ball in case the keeper parries it back towards him. He can't kick it for a second time if it rebounds from the goal until another player has touched it.

TAKING CORNERS

' Goalkeeping seems to have developed to such an extent that the old-fashioned corner is no longer much use. A cross simply hit into the penalty area will nowadays be cut out by the keeper. Attacking sides are using the flick-on header at the near-post. But no doubt someone will come up with another successful variation when this idea has been cancelled out by defences '

The corner is possibly the one area of the game which has developed more than any other in recent years. Not so long ago the idea behind a corner was simply to take a free kick from the quadrant area that's marked off in the corner of the pitch. The taker would float his cross into the centre of the penalty area hoping that a colleague would 'get on the end of it'. But defenders and goalkeepers began to win this battle, and corner-kicking has changed as tactics have matured.

The most dangerous ploy to be used by an attacking side now is probably to place a good aerial player on the near post to back-head the ball from somewhere around the six-yard box, and suddenly change the 'shape' of the corner by either directing the ball sideways to a colleague, or over the goalkeeper to the far post.

The kicker has to hit the ball into the six-yard

box with a lot of pace and just above head height, so that the players in his side who've gone onto the near post can get a touch.

Dangerous deflections
One of the reasons why this move has proved so successful has been the additional opportunities it creates from a corner, plus the chance that the attack might be helped by an unwilling touch by a defender.

A defender might be tempted to get his head to the cross in an effort to knock the ball away from the danger zone, but if the ball is out of his reach he can play the part the attacker was hoping to fulfil by deflecting the ball across his own goal!

The attack should be looking for one or two of their players to set off on a run towards the far post and the centre of goal from positions outside the penalty area, as the kick is being taken.

Provided that the corner-taker is accurate with his cross, and the near-post man is able to deflect the ball over the top of the defenders coming in from behind him, he'll create a scoring opportunity for the runners. It's their aim to get to the ball as it reaches the front of the goal towards the far post, where they have a chance of a strike.

Perhaps it's because goalkeepers have improved (I'm sure they'd like to know I've said that anyway) but to me the ball simply centred into the six-yard box is useless. It's a 'keeper's ball' and any goalkeeper worth his salt will snap it up — at any level.

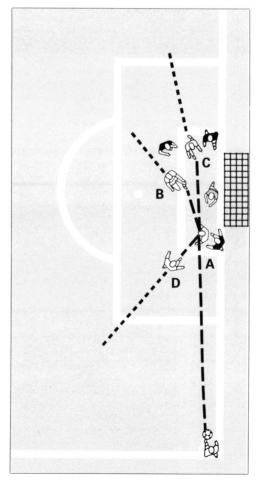

The near post corner: Player **A** is the target man for this type of corner. He can head on to players **B** and **C** who are running into the goal area or down to player **D** coming in on the nearpost.

ROBSON'S TIPS

● *Corner-takers should practise striking different length crosses accurately. A corner can be just as dangerous if played to a colleague running in from a strong position as it is floated into the goalmouth.*

● *A corner is a free kick and should be used by the attacking side to gain advantage of the dead ball. It's up to the defence to organize itself to cover all scoring possibilities.*

● *The short corner is one way of pulling defenders out of the penalty area to cover the extra man involved and it can give the attacking side more space in the box.*

A direct free kick

You should always remember that a corner is a direct free kick, and it's therefore possible to score straight from a dead-ball. But the chances of doing this are slim, especially if the team you're playing against has a well organized defence.

Sometimes on a windy day you can cause serious problems for your opponents if you're able to float the ball in from just above the near post. This is a very difficult cross for the goalkeeper to deal with and he might even palm the ball into his own net!

The accuracy and ability of the kicker is always a vital point to be taken into consideration. If he has the power to drive the ball to the far post, and the skill to drop it on a small target, then he's of great value to any set-up.

At first the distance between corner flag and the near post can seem formidable to a young player and that's why junior games are usually played on smaller pitches, but it's surprising how soon you can master the art of crossing a long ball with practice. Even so, young players have the option of various ploys if there isn't a strong corner-taker in the side.

The short corner

One of the favourite moves among teams who have a player with an exceptionally strong shot is to play a corner into his path so that he can meet the ball on the run around the angle of the penalty area.

His drive may well be blocked if the defence is covering the goalmouth, but there are possibilities of a deflection, a rebound to an attacking player in a scoring position, or even an 'in-off'.

Another ploy often used in this type of situation is for the player running into the edge of the box to slip the ball to the far post. With the defence covering the near post and preparing for the flick-on, the ball is laid to the player coming in from midfield and his chip is aimed at the angle above the head of the far-post defender. If the ball is hit well enough, and weighted so that it drops just below the crossbar, the possibilities of scoring are high. The keeper will have been covering the near-post cross and could be unsighted by the bodies in the box, while the dropping ball will be out of the reach of the defence.

In the 1950s the short corner really became popular. Before that the most popular ploy was just to bang the ball into the middle of the box around the penalty spot, but with the game's tactical development new ideas were tried out.

One of them was to use two players around the corner quadrant. The idea was that by putting two players around the ball defenders will be pulled out of the penalty area to cover, leaving the attackers in the box with more space.

This has been used to good effect by many teams and is another variation of the corner, which after all should always present opponents with a problem to solve. If the player assisting at the corner can run for the goal-line with the ball, and his colleague cut inside after taking the short kick, the twin attack can face the defence with a difficult situation, one which could end in a shot at target.

Above left: The short corner — I take the corner and immediately run behind the receiver who was standing close to me on the touchline.

Above right: The marker — who has to be ten yards away when the kick is taken — closes in but with two players to cover is not certain who will make the attacking move.

DECIDING TACTICS

❝ I think that unqualified coaches should make sure they don't try to teach young players to do things the wrong way. There's nothing worse than when a youngster joins a club and finds out that he's been doing something basic in totally the wrong way because he's been shown the incorrect method by a so-called coach. Let the young kids enjoy their soccer – there's plenty of time for tactics later ❞

Below left: Man-to-man marking is one of the most frustrating tactics used by some European sides. It's normally used with the sweeper system.

Below right: Mobility and dummy runs to draw an opponent away from a colleague can create an opening even against the most disciplined defence.

The tactics used during a game of soccer can be as varied as the skills of the players involved, but today strategy is as important as the ability of individuals. A good all-round team, disciplined and playing to its strengths, can get the better of a group of highly talented individuals who 'play it by ear'.

The teams of today have found it possible to eliminate the threat of a highly skilled player by using a pattern that has been created to make the best of the talent available. Of course, if you couple high standards of skill with the correct tactics you can create tremendous teams. Liverpool play to their strength of being a 'passing' team with good players in their line-up and they've become successful thanks to the combination of skill and a well-planned formula.

To me the Liverpool method is the way that soccer should be played: accurate passing, strong support in attack and defence, good use of the ball at all times, and a combination of skill and well-planned tactics.

Short and long styles
Other clubs use different ideas. Everton try to pass the ball as much as possible but they also hit the ball forward early to get their strikers going, making their approach a combination of two styles.

Sheffield Wednesday and Watford are totally different. Their method is to get the ball forward as early as possible when they can and let their front men chase, and while this might suit their

players I don't think that it helps at international level.

If club sides are playing to a pattern that's far removed from anything being used by others, then their players find it hard when they have to re-adapt to more familiar systems. I'm sure that revolutionary styles can handicap players when they're called up by their national side.

And that brings me to the national teams who have their own tactics. Most sides from mainland Europe play 'man-to-man' marking with a 'sweeper', and while some English clubs have experimented with this method the majority stick to what they know best – marking zones or areas in defence with no extra men behind them.

The sweeper has a free role and this extra man in defence makes it difficult for forwards, but since it means that other members of the opposition are given space to run from midfield it's essential that everyone understands the tactics being used.

Junior sides should *not* use tactics. I believe youngsters should get out and enjoy their soccer without being disciplined to playing to a certain pattern. I know it's essential that players stick to the position they're supposed to be filling, but if a defender sees that there's a chance of going forward then he should go – and if the defence is under pressure then it's up to the others to help out.

Playing for fun
The majority of people play soccer for fun, not

for a living, and that's why they should get the most possible out of it.

Young players should never be stopped from enjoying their game. Kids should be trying as many skills on the ball as they can – without any circus tricks! If players try a bit of skill and it comes off that's fine so long as they don't overdo it. They must always remember that they're part of a team. If you try a trick and it comes off only once out of ten attempts you aren't really helping your colleagues. The golden rule is: keep it simple.

At the same time people in charge of youngsters, whether they are teachers or just volunteers who help out with junior teams or scout groups should remember that coaching is for the experts. There are many young boys who are taught certain things by so-called coaches and when they get themselves with a club find out that they have been doing everything wrong.

Nothing annoys me more than to hear about teams of very young players being told by the person in charge that they should be playing to a certain pattern. While I realize that it's essential that players understand the basic requirements of their role during a game it's also important for the people who are trying to teach them to have some idea of what they are talking about.

Developing skills

I feel that players under 13 or so should be left to enjoy the game, learn by their mistakes and get some pleasure out of developing their playing skills.

Nowadays in music there are lots of children who get pleasure out of learning to play an instrument and much of the theory has been removed from the early stages. Once they've had the pleasure of making a few tunes from a simple guide they're led into music as a pleasure.

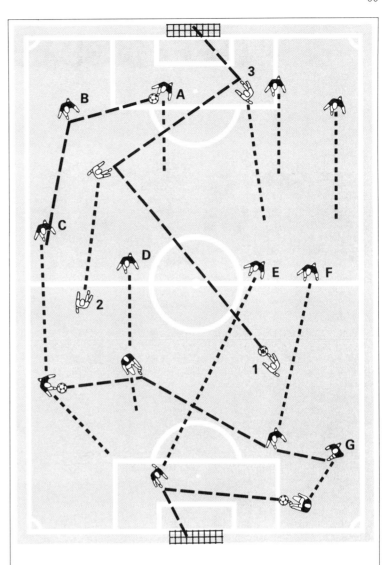

Two contrasting uses of tactics (numbers, the long ball; letters, the build-up from defence): The long ball: Player **1** passes a diagonal long ball forward to player **2** who has run from midfield. He carries the ball a very short distance before crossing for **3** to score. The opposition will try to use the offside trap to counteract this type of play. Building from defence: this method uses many more players and involves keeping possession. **A** plays to **B** who passes to **C**. He plays inside to **D** and continues on a decoy run. Player **E** goes on a diagonal run behind the ball as **F** comes in from the left, collects and plays to **G**. He runs to the edge of the penalty area and plays a cross into the path of **E** who is now running in towards the far post. Other supporting players are in positions to help out if the move falls down.

━ ━ Path of ball
■ ■ ■ Path of player

That same rule should apply to soccer. Players should be given the chance to pick up the basics and develop those skills before being asked to think too seriously about tactics.

Once they have made the grade, and joined the 'orchestra' then expert tuition can guide them into new areas of enjoyment.

DEFENSIVE TACTICS

'Defenders have to play as a team. They must work for each other and help out. If the right-back is going in to challenge, the right-sided central defender should be up there as well, making sure that if the ball comes loose he'll get it. But not only that: the left-sided central defender should be helping him, and the left-back should be covering too! A good defence is a constantly moving outfit – talking, shouting and checking on each other all the time'

Right: As the attacker runs down the left flank I cover my full-back by moving into his zone.

Far right: The attacker turns inside away from the full-back but momentarily loses control, giving me the opportunity to steal the ball because of good backing up. If the attacker had beaten this cover another defender would enter the zone as his colleagues recovered.

The secret of any good defence is to have a group of players who all 'work for each other'. If one player is on the ball or marking a man who's in possession, then the defending side has to cover all possible areas that the player can run to or the ball can be played.

Support is the keyword for defenders just as it is for attackers. And while the same rule can apply for the attack it's most important for the players at the back because if they fail to help out their side can go a goal down.

Perhaps it would help if I explained more fully the zonal cover scheme I've mentioned earlier. If you were to imagine that the defence's half of the field was divided into a grid and this stretched from the goal-line up to the halfway line in four roughly equal sections, it would give an idea of the zone each man in the back four has to look after.

But there's more to it than that. Players can't just run up and down in an imaginary rectangle and never come out of it!

No, the idea behind zonal cover gives the back four its guidelines for blocking out the opposition's attack. But they have to move around to cover the whole of their half. They do this by operating as a unit rather than as a group of individuals, with each one helping out the others.

Working the zonal system

Going back to our grid: if we can picture a situation where the opposition winger has the ball on *our* right I can give you some idea of how to use the zontal system as part of your defensive tactics.

Let's call this far right-hand zone the red zone, next to it the blue, then the green and finally the yellow. The ball is *always* in a red zone and the areas change colour so that blue is always next to red, green next to blue and yellow is the zone farthest away from the ball when we can use all four colours.

When the ball is on our right the right full-back is responsible for this area so he's gone to cover the player with the ball. The right-sided central defender is in a blue zone. He has got to back up, cover any opponent trying to make a run into his

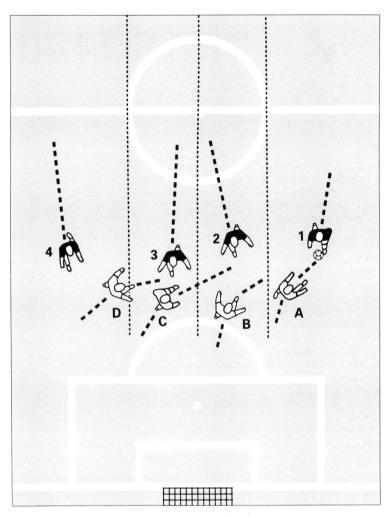

area while at the same time being in a position to pick up the ball if his full-back makes a challenge and the ball breaks free.

The left-sided central defender has moved to the edge of the green and into the blue, while the left-back can leave the yellow zone and move inside to cover the green. There should be no danger from the attack's right (the defence's left) because of the distance the ball has to travel from the other flank. A long pass would allow the defenders time to reposition themselves.

Backing up

If the winger is able to get the ball to a man on the inside then the second zone becomes the red area. The winger is in the blue, and the left-sided central defender is also in a blue zone with the yellow changing to green and needing some cover because it's closer to play and any opponent in that area will need to be marked.

Of course during a game you cannot stop to think about coloured zones and whether or not the ball has crossed into a section that's your responsibility or not. The idea of that example was to illustrate how the back four men have to back each other up and form a solid defence.

If a winger was so skilled that he was able to beat player after player and the system is being applied to the letter, the defenders would be moving across to cover in such a way that the winger would pass first the right full-back, then the right-sided central defender, then the left-sided, then the left-back. But it would be no consolation for the manager!

Actually if a player did do this sort of thing and did beat the four defenders it would show that the defence was operating properly, even though they had failed to win the ball. If the opponent had pushed the ball too far for close control, however, the run would have ended when one of the defenders picked it up as he came to support.

Cover every option

The best 'back fours' are those who know what each other will do, talk to their colleagues during

the game and keep getting themselves into the correct positions. They've also got to cover the edge of the penalty area and not let forwards make runs there without the risk of being caught offside, and to make sure that they're on the shoulder of the player moving up to challenge.

But defenders should also remember that they must not stand still. They can't watch play going on in the other half of the field. They've got to move up too so that if the opposition put anyone upfield they can catch them offside.

Ideally, when the defenders' side is on the attack one of the full-backs should have moved upfield to join in, the two central defenders should have closed the area around the halfway line and the other back gone into a space where he can cut out any long ball played out by the opposition which might catch them unawares.

You must call to each other when defending and organizing yourselves so that you cover every option. Even though their side might have possession, the defence should still be prepared for the moment when the opposition win the ball again and make sure they have their players marked.

Never make it easy for the other team to attack.

Zonal cover: Player **1** has the ball out on the attack's left wing. Defender **A** moves in to challenge with **B** backing up to cover the tackle and cut off a pass inside to **2**. Defender **C** runs into the zone to his right to cut out a pass to **2** or **3** and **D** covers for **C** leaving **4** unmarked but out of the move.

■ ■ ■ ■ Path of player

THE OFFSIDE TRAP

❝ The offside trap can be effective, but I hate to see teams using it all the time. If that's the way that you play regularly then you're going to get caught out. Opponents quickly find out that teams use the offside trap a lot, so they instruct their players to hold the ball and run at the defence. I certainly know from watching teams who overuse it that it spoils the game for the spectators ❞

There are many ways to prevent the opposition from attacking your goal, and one of the most common tactics is to use the offside trap. This is exactly what its name implies – a trap to catch the opposing side in an offside position by an organized movement of the defence.

Players will be caught offside during normal play. A forward will stray into a position where, if the ball is played by one of his colleagues, he'll be ruled to be offside. The trap is to make sure that the defence gets a free kick by forcing the attack into an area they had no real intention of occupying.

Don't overdo it

It's a good defensive ploy, but kids should never overdo it, though in junior soccer deliberately playing an opponent offside is rare.

To explain what happens is simple. First you have to understand what being offside means. If there are fewer than two opponents between an attacker and the goal-line in the opposition half of the field at the time the ball is played forward by a member of the attacking team the attacker is offside.

I said it was simple but I know some fans don't really understand the rules, which also say that if the attacker is level with the second of the two defenders he is still offside. Most spectators watch the ball, not the attacker. In the split-second their eyes move to him, he's moved offside – and they start booing the linesman!

The offside trap makes sure that as the ball is

played forward, the defence moves out in a line to leave the attacker stranded goalside, with just the goalkeeper between him and the goal-line . . . in other words he's caught!

A solid line

Teams who play the offside trap tend to play very square in defence; they have to move up in a solid line to make it work.

Right: Beating the offside trap. I time my run to pick up a return pass from my team-mate who stays in front of his marker to remain on-side.

Centre right: As I run wide the ball is played into my path and even though the defence moves forward I've beaten the trap.

Far right: The deep defender watching my team-mate has given the attacking side the opportunity to break through.

At United we've caught Liverpool out many times over the years when they've tried to use their offside trap on us. The way to beat the trap is to move your forwards out with the opposing defence, as the midfield men run through with the ball. The defence is expecting a through-ball to the forwards but instead a good one-two in midfield opens up the gap at the back and your midfield man is free to go at the target.

To make the trap work requires the full-backs to push up slightly in front of the two central defenders, and it's these 'middle men' who spring the trap. If the team in possession go to play the ball forward and the striker runs in behind the full-back on either side, the centre-back lets him go and moves up as the ball is played: the player is caught.

The golden rule is for the centre-back to watch where his other defenders are or he can be in trouble. It's no use him springing the trap if the others aren't ready, for all he does is take himself out of the game by moving upfield as the attack gets in behind him.

Beating the trap

One thing every player should get into his head is that you can't be offside if you keep dribbling the ball downfield, and I've often seen good ball players beating the trap just like that.

They pick up a pass on the halfway line and as their colleagues run into position the defence works to its system of moving out at the moment they expect the player in possession to play the ball forward. Instead he keeps on running, beating the challenge and the trap at the same time, and getting himself into the danger zone.

This type of move can often lead to a goal because the defence has moved out square, left space at the back with nobody to cover the goalkeeper and it's one player against another. It can, of course, be ruined by another attacker being caught offside, even though he may not actually be 'interfering with play'.

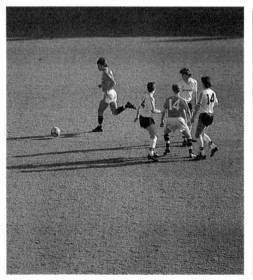

Top: Springing the trap – as the attacker comes downfield the defence moves forward in a 'square' position.
Centre: As a defender moves in to challenge, his team-mates press forward leaving the attacker caught offside.
Bottom: Even if the attacker had stayed in line with the defence he would have fallen for the ploy. Defenders have to learn to move out at the precise moment the trap is about to be sprung.

BUILDING THE WALL

❝ The wall's a fairly modern innovation, probably because before the 1960s not many players could bend a free kick the way that they can today. The lighter ball has had a lot to do with teams lining players up to block direct shots, and now it's put up for anything up to 30 yards away from goal ❞

Below left: A three-man wall has been formed for a free kick outside the penalty area. I push into the end of the wall to worry the defence. Will the attack shoot at me because I'm going to move or will they use another set piece?
Below right: The goalkeeper's view. He has covered his near post with the wall but is uncertain if the opponent in the wall will move so has a greater possibility of being beaten.

The defensive wall at free kicks is one of the most familiar sights in the modern game. It's been developed as a tactical method of preventing a direct shot at goal, and used properly it can be very effective.

It's really up to the goalkeeper to decide how many players he wants in his wall, and this can range from three to as many as seven. I've even seen a photograph of an entire team lined up along a goal-line for an indirect free kick inside their penalty area, but thankfully this is a fairly rare sight!

The theory behind the wall is that by placing a number of men in a line in front of the kicker he'll have little chance of getting a fierce shot on target. This is true in most cases, although taking free kicks is developing just like many other areas of the game, and the experts at set pieces will always be on the lookout for a way of outwitting the opposition.

Solid – but not linked

A fairly straightforward method of forming a wall is for the outer player – the one farthest away from the centre of the goal – to stand in an area in line with the near post, and for the other members of the wall to close up to him. They should not link arms.

If players do link then they'll find themselves in trouble if the ball is knocked short to the side of them, for they'll be tugging and pulling at each other so much the opposition will be onto the ball before they've broken loose.

You should always remember to have at least one 'spare' man lining up alongside the wall to cover the break around the back. Talking of breaking, the wall must *never* break. The whole idea of it being there is to stop the ball, and even if it happens to hit you it won't hurt that much.

Defenders in the wall must not duck out of the way of the ball even if it's blasted straight at them. If it's coming at head height, get your forehead to it and head it clear. If it comes at your body you can chest it down. Hold your hands in front of you and they'll act as protection for your stomach, groin and upper thighs.

Arrange the wall quickly, perhaps with one player facing the keeper as he directs the group of players to the left or right, indicating with his hand signals where he wants it to stop. Then the player in the wall should turn and face the kicker and all the defenders in the wall must brace themselves for the shot – at the same time being ready for the unexpected.

This might be a little push a few yards past the outside edge of the wall for a player to run on to, and the defenders in the wall must break to close him down. This is the only time when the wall breaks – when the ball is played away from it.

I mentioned earlier the player on the loose and his job is always to attack the ball at the free kick, especially if it's rolled to the side for the secondary attacker to have a shot at goal. The quicker he is to anticipate the approach being used by the opposition the more chance he will have of cutting out the danger.

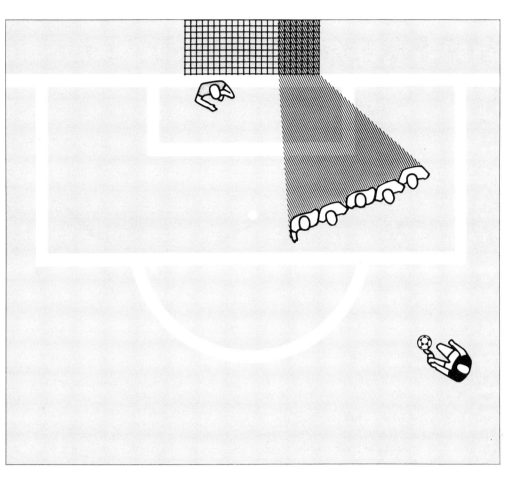

The wall: Here five men cover an area from the near post to a quarter of the way across goal. The keeper guards the other area but an additional defender could increase the wall's cover. The attack might try to chip over the wall towards the near post and the defence must be prepared for this.

Tipping the scales

While the attack has a slight edge at set pieces, the operation of an effective wall and a massed defence should tip the scales back a little towards the opposition. They are facing upfield and have time to organize themselves in such a way that most angles are covered. This is perhaps why managers are often angry when a goal's given away at a set piece, and if it's come over or through the wall they find it hard to forgive!

One of the advantages that top players have over those in junior soccer is that we usually know a bit about the opposition. By that I mean that before the game the manager can say to us that we are responsible for picking up a certain player at free kicks and corners, and we know what's wanted from us because we know who the player is.

But when you're playing against a team of players you've never seen before it can make things a bit difficult.

The way round this is for coaches to make players responsible for certain areas of the defence. If a wall has to be formed he will tell certain players that it's their duty to be in it. He needs a sharp, quick tackler to stay loose, and probably a couple of tall men to look after the opposition's strikers, who are going to threaten from the edge of the box by running in.

Most of all, the coach's instructions must be for everybody to be on their toes at set pieces, because it's up to the defence to win back the advantage they have lost by giving away the free kick – and perhaps break out quickly into attack themselves.

MARKING YOUR OPPONENT

❝ Zonal marking is the most popular system in England. That's where each of the back four is responsible for approximately a quarter of the field in the defence's half. If the ball is on the right, the four will move across that way, each playing off their team-mate's shoulder and prepared to leave an opponent free if he's on the opposite side of the field to the ball. But if play is switched they have time to swing cover to that side ❞

The secret of good marking is to remember that you should always be 'goal side' of your player. The goal you're defending is on the opposite side of your body from the player you're watching.

This means that you can at times even allow the player to take control of the ball knowing that you'll be able to organize yourself to make the challenge, yet your goal will be safe.

The object of any defender must be to make sure that the opposition doesn't get between him and the goal; if he does, he'll find that he's up against the same sort of snags that the forward has if he stays on the correct side.

Playing between the opponent and the goal means that for the attacking player to control the ball, receive a pass or advance, he has first got to turn (because the ball will be coming to him from upfield), fend off your challenge, and *then* get past you. The defender has the advantage every time.

The idea of marking an opponent means that you're in direct opposition to him. You must try to prevent him from gaining any sort of advantage, but he'll also be trying his hardest to see that he gets the upper hand.

The sin of ball-watching

One of the biggest faults I've seen when watching schoolboy soccer – and by this I mean at ordinary school level, not international standard – is that the players tend to 'ball-watch' during the game.

If a pass comes in from the wing the defenders

will tend to converge on the ball, and not watch what is happening around them. The winger can be finding himself space out wide, or more importantly other players could be running into attacking positions on the 'blind-side', but still the young defenders tend to watch only the player with the ball.

Good markers don't ball watch; they look for the space that is being created by the attacking move and close it down, or wait for the moment

Right: An opponent approaches in possession with a colleague supporting. I'm holding off my challenge but running towards the player with the ball.

Centre right: I've placed myself to the attacker's left making him push the ball wide and cutting out the possibility of a pass to the support player.

Far right: The player has run wide and can only turn inside so the challenge is timed for the moment he is not in total control.

that the pass is made and try to intercept.

I've got to stress that 'ball-watching' and 'watching the ball' are two very different things. Watching the ball is essential when you are about to play it, or make a tackle. But when you are covering in defence you must be aware of what is going on around you and ready to anticipate the next move . . . not watching the ball!

During top level games you'll sometimes see players left out on their own, apparently unmarked, but you can more or less guarantee that they won't be. Whoever is responsible for marking them will be in a position to cut out any threat from them, while still covering another part of the action.

An exception was the Portuguese goal against England in Mexico in 1986 – the whole back four (and not just Gary Stevens) were guilty of watching only the player with the ball and not his team-mates.

Man-to-man-to-man-to-man marking! Five Newcastle players cover me as they get a bit carried away with defensive cover.

SOCCER SYSTEMS

❝ In countries where clubs use the sweeper system – with perhaps the exception of Italy and Spain – crowds are getting smaller. In England while attendances may have fallen off over the years there are still much bigger gates than in general in mainland Europe. That may say something about the way the crowds feel about the type of soccer they get served up with **❞**

Once upon a time there were two full-backs, three half-backs and five forwards. No, it isn't a fairy tale or even an old soccer story; that was the way that the game started off.

The formation used by teams for many years was what we would call 2-3-5. This meant that up front there were two wingers, two inside-forwards, and a centre-forward; behind them was a centre-half and two wing-halves, one left and the other right. At the back came the two full-backs. In the period between the two world wars the centre-half moved back to a position between the full-backs and the two inside-forwards adopted more of a midfield role. If you draw this on a piece of paper – and then link up the dots – you get the 'W-M' figure which gave the pattern its name. In the late 1950s one of the wing-halves became defensive to create the 'back four' we know today.

All my soccer has been 4-2-4, 4-4-2 or 4-3-3, which are the most popular systems used nowadays. But I've seen teams when they've played away from home putting four men at the back, five in midfield and leaving just one man up front. They've come to defend and stop the opposition from scoring rather than going for goal themselves.

I've also seen five at the back, three in midfield, and two up front as they've looked for a way of breaking down the opposition and still be in with a chance of scoring themselves.

Working for each other

The whole idea of the modern game is to have players working for each other. In 4-4-2 and 4-2-4 the principle is the same with the wide players working back to help out in midfield, or in the case of 4-4-2 moving up to put pressure on the defence – the opposition's I mean!

The systems work by having four players across the defence, and these players push forward when their colleagues are on the attack becoming the midfield, while the midfield four have joined the two front runners to make a temporary six-player attack.

From the opposite angle the two midfield players out wide will move back to increase the number of players in the opponent's defence and try to cancel out the extra attackers.

The wide players have got to work very hard to make these systems work, but top clubs have used them for years and proved them successful.

Clubs have used a sweeper behind the back four to give them more solidarity in defence but it

can hinder them in attack. I think that's one of the reasons why the sweeper system has not really caught on in the English game. Other Europeans have got used to it because it developed in Europe, but English crowds seem to find it boring and frustrating when they see a side playing with a sweeper.

After 4-4-2 and 4-2-4, the next most popular system used in our game is 4-3-3. This gives a side four players across the back and three midfielders, with one playing wide in the front three and two strikers. It has got to be made clear to any young player that systems are styles of play, *not* barriers to him enjoying his soccer. The same applies to the people in charge of junior teams. It's no use them saying that they will use a particular system if the players they have are unsuitable for it. If a club has two fast, skilful wingers it's no use playing 4-3-3 or one of them is going to be back in midfield.

Keeping it simple

Tactics can confuse young players and trying to make a group of small boys play to a strict system can only make matters worse. They don't need to be told that they are playing 4-2-4 or any other pattern – just encouraged to carry out their role as a defender, a striker or a creator in midfield and allowed to get the most out of the game.

The systems can come later.

Obviously when you play the game at the level I've reached it's a different story, but I've come across some strange systems I can tell you!

Nine-man defences

This has usually been when I have played abroad with England, or against foreign sides at Wembley. I've seen sides leaving just one player up front and pulling the rest back in defence because they've expected England to beat them. This type of system can be really hard to break down because there are always nine players behind the ball.

At times like this is doesn't matter how much talent you have in your side; if the opposition is simply trying to stop you from scoring, and has no real intention of going forward, you've got problems.

The danger is that you can pull your own defenders out of position, piling players into the opposition's half. Then, if you lose possession, you're a sitting duck for the breakaway.

I remember watching Greece at Wembley after England had beaten them 3-0 in their country.

Soccer formations:
A 2-3-5, used for many years since before the Second World War
B 'W-M', in which the midfield players linked with defence and attack.
C A sweeper plays behind the back four with three men in midfield and two strikers.
D 4-3-3, used by many modern-day clubs.
E 4-2-4, an attacking style of play.

ROBSON'S TIPS

● *You adapt the system to suit the players, not the players to suit the system.*

● *A good manager tells each individual player what he expects of him during a game. Players should be made aware of their role and not simply told what system the side is using.*

● *When playing against a side which is playing with a high number of men in defence don't be drawn into the trap of sending too many players into their half. This leaves openings at the back and gives them the chance of a breakaway.*

They came to England to defend and left just one player up near the halfway line while the others packed the back. The game ended in a draw 0-0, but I could see why we had problems.

The danger was that our defenders would get pulled into 'false positions' because Greece had so many players back. If we left two players up near the halfway line to watch the lone striker we had to be careful not to move our other back-four players too far inside or this would leave openings for the breakaway. What you're left with is a team of nine players and a goalkeeper defending against six or eight others and that's why it's so hard to crack that system . . . and it's terrible to watch!

Regular systems
During my days at West Brom we usually played 4-3-3 with either Willie Johnston or Laurie Cunningham as the one winger, with Ally Brown and Cyrille Regis up front and three midfield players. That was our regular system, and when Laurie and Willie played in the same team we would switch to two wide players, which was quite effective.

At United we have always tried to play with two wide players, but when Arnold Muhren was in the team we played with four midfield players.

For England we played 4-2-4 for a while with Mark Chamberlain and John Barnes on the wings, but I think that at international level managers prefer four players in midfield. The reason for this is the standard of midfield play in the opposition, and you need that extra defender in there to try to close these players down.

But no matter what the level, it's no use a manger just saying 'we'll play 4-2-4 today'. He has to issue instructions to each player about what he expects from him, who he wants him to cover, what area of the field he wants him to play in, and how he wants him to help out in others. That's what makes the system work.

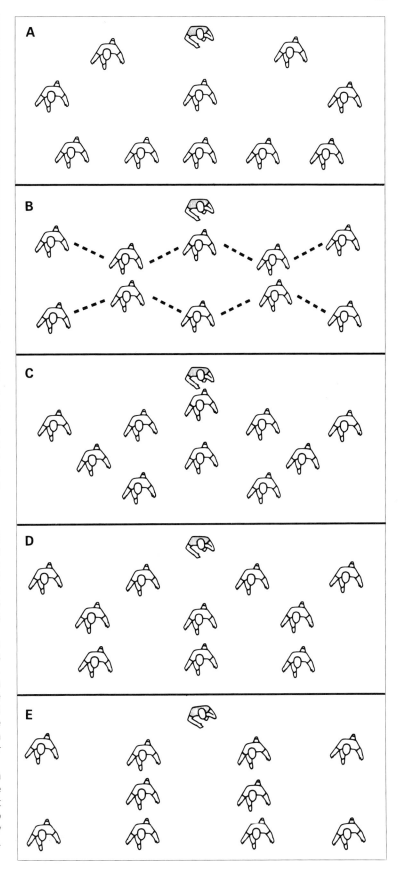

ATTACKING TACTICS

❝ Attacking is the whole idea of soccer. You want to score goals and the only way to do this is to attack the opposition's goal. You won't score every time you go up the field, but you must try to make each attack count with a final shot towards the target. Supporters watching top-level soccer will go home satisfied with a goalless draw if they've seen both teams trying to score yet cancelling each other out. If nobody ever gets a decent shot on target then the game has been a waste of time ❞

Manchester United's style of play is to use two 'wide players' in attack, and I feel that this is the way most clubs should tackle the game. It broadens the front line so that players can get into good positions inside, and it also means that by using players out wide you're incorporating most of the playing area into your game.

Spreading your attack across the pitch creates more openings than a narrower approach. The wide men can get past full-backs and create scoring chances by getting down into the danger zone – that strip of the field about ten yards up from the goal-line, and down to the line itself.

This was introduced to put the centre of the opposition's team under pressure from the beginning of the game. It pulls men out of position early on and gives you the advantage of moving up straight away.

Attack from the start

The basics of attacking tactics are to get players into spaces where they can create problems for the defence. Using the *width* I referred to at the start of this section gives teams the chance of pulling defenders out of the box and this creates the openings for the strikers to make their runs.

What young players must always remember is that attackers need *support*. Thus you also need *depth* in attack. If you are a defender then you should be ready to move upfield to help out, closing down on the opposition and getting your back players up to the halfway line to cover the breakout, and win back the ball played in your direction from an opposition clearance.

I could go on for ever about the different ways that teams try to break down the opposition, but the most common is for the wide runner to carry the ball down the flank and either cross into the penalty area or pull it back to a supporting player coming into the space behind.

You can go on the attack right from the kick-off and many clubs use a system United adopted when Mark Hughes was at Old Trafford. This is to send a strong fast forward wide on the right, or the left, and put the opposition under pressure from the moment that the referee signals the start of play.

In the centre circle the player kicking off rolls the ball forward a short distance, his support player takes over and knocks it back to a midfielder who's coming up from behind and at the same time the two players involved in the kick-off spread left and right.

As soon as the whistle has blown the strong forward has gone on a run down the wing and he's now in front of the full-back. The midfielder plays a long ball down the wing in a diagonal line over the top of the full-back, forcing him to turn, and at the same time the forward challenges for the ball. If he wins it he will be behind the back with space to move into the danger zone and his colleagues will be running into positions around goal.

The idea behind the move is to get you into the opposition's half of the field and put pressure on them immediately. By using Mark's strength and speed we were often able to create an early opening, and this is a tactic used regularly by Everton.

When I've played with England we have also tried this early wing attack, but another idea that Bobby Robson has used is the direct attack down the middle. This was introduced to put pressure on the centre of the opposition's team from the off. It pulls men out of position early on and gives you the advantage of moving up straight away.

From the kick-off teams are cautious of the approach the side playing the ball might use. If you've tried putting a player wide on past occasions then the run at the defence from the centre might create space, especially if the opposition is expecting you to use the long ball wide.

Varying the pattern

I suppose this is a single illustration of what coaches mean by never assuming that teams will play to a fixed pattern all the time. Players are trying to outwit each other, and coaches are always thinking up ways of applying pressure; and of course ways of making sure that their defenders can cope with the schemes being used by their rivals.

Soccer is a game of opportunity. If the chance of a goal comes and it means deviating from the pattern you've been trying to play, I doubt if any coach will have you up in front of the mananger on Monday morning for scoring the winner!

At the same time the reason that tactics play such an important part in professional soccer is that the game is so well organized that if a side plays without a system it will quickly find that it has problems against a team that does. If each member of a team knows at any given time what to expect from his colleagues – where to run, where to play the ball, if he'll have support and so on – they will have the advantage over an outfit that improvises all the time.

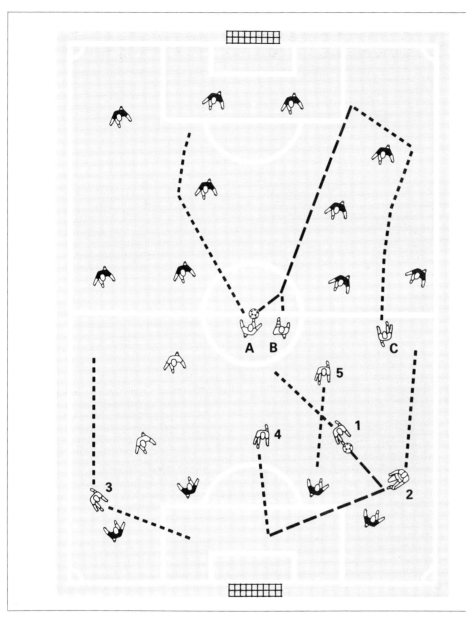

Top: Using a strong runner down the flank: From the kick-off **A** rolls the ball forward to **B** and immediately runs through the defence to the left of the penalty area. At the kick-off **C** has run down the flank and behind the full-back. The ball is played into this space by **B** before the defence can close in.

Bottom: Two wide players – one a decoy – attack down the flanks: **1** carries the ball diagonally forward as **5** draws a defender by running across behind the player in possession. **2** and **3** advance, drawing defenders and **4** sees an opening down the centre. The ball is played to **2** who crosses into the path of **4** to strike.

▬ ▬   Path of ball
▪ ▪ ▪   Path of player

Liverpool always seem to try to keep possession. They play the ball back and hold it. They seem to believe that everybody in the side should have an early touch on the ball, and are quite willing to let the opposition get into their half of the field because they feel they are capable of coping with this pressure as long as they have the ball. Nobody could argue that this system doesn't work, but to be successful it requires the high standard of skill and practice Liverpool have in their players and training methods.

Junior clubs shouldn't concern themselves too much with sophisticated tactics, but keep the game simple. Pass from player to player, move into space ready for the one-two, and cover the breakaways at the back. It sounds straightforward, doesn't it? Well, soccer is a simple game, you know!

ROBSON'S TIPS

- *Adapt your tactics to the strengths of your team. If you have fast players out wide, use them to break down defences.*

- *Remember that an accurate pass for a colleague to run on to is the simplest way of beating an opponent.*

- *The top clubs have their own particular styles of attacking. See which one is closest to your side's style of play and see if there are any moves you can adopt and adapt – but keep it simple!*

BEATING THE WALL

❛ Some clubs use a signalling method from free kicks where the taker raises one hand above his head if he's going to play the ball to the near post, then two if he means the far post. Then they'll try to fool the opposition by raising two when they're playing to the near. It's all 'kidology' really – but if *you* know what *you're* going to do, then let the opposition worry **❜**

Set-piece play really concerns the last third of the field. It involves the tactics used by an attacking side which has been given the advantage of dictating how play should continue from a corner or a free kick.

A set piece is a rehearsed move, something that a team has been able to practise during training. At the top level I can assure you that a great deal of attention is given to this type of play.

It's possible from a set piece to create an opening against the best defences provided that things go according to plan, but like every other part of the game things would be very easy if it were not for the opposition!

The set piece ought to give the attack the edge because for once during play the players on one team know exactly what *should* happen. I stress the word 'should' because a set-piece move is no out-and-out guarantee that a goal will be scored.

It does give the attacking side the chance to put players in advantageous positions in the opponents' half of the field, and until the referee indicates that the free kick or corner has to be taken, there's very little that the defence can do apart from mark up.

Variations on a theme

For a simple example let's take a free kick just outside the penalty area on the attack's left side. The taker has positioned the ball and the defence has formed a 'wall' of players between the ball and the near post. The goalkeeper is covering an area of goal to the right of the wall. It's now up to the attacking side to get a shot at goal and apart from the direct drive, which could be a curving shot around the wall, or straight at it hoping that it will break, the kicker might choose to chip – or use the planned set-piece play.

There are so many variations I could probably fill the pages of this book with different set-piece moves I've seen, but we're looking for a way through the defence; and once the ball is kicked the advantage is there to be won or lost.

A blind run by a player close to the kicker (giving the impression that the ball will be played to him) can pull a player out of the wall or a defender out of the penalty area leaving space for the shot; a chip to an area above the six-yard box on the opposite side of the goalmouth from the wall can create an aerial opportunity for a player running in; a chip in the other direction may give a runner an opening behind the wall which will have to turn to cover.

Creating space

The attack has got to try to create space in the box. A striker can be just as dangerous running away from play as he can running towards it. If this type of ploy is used it will pull a big central defender out of the way because he'll follow the striker and this might leave space for another player to move in.

As I've said the variations are endless and teams can use combinations of different set pieces to gain an advantage, never using the same trick twice during a game.

It can become complicated so it's essential that all the players involved know exactly what's expected from them and run into the correct positions.

Using a runner

I think that a rule which should always apply for any set piece is to have a player running from behind the ball when you are attacking. By doing this you take away any possibility of him being marked at the time the kick's taken – but the defence should have someone ready to pick him up to try to counter the move.

Whether he actually plays the ball or not isn't that important; the fact that the runner has been used means that the defence can't simply cover to block a shot. They have to watch the player coming from behind the ball as well as the kicker.

This leads me to another tactic often used at free kicks close to goal. If two or more players line up with the ball in front of them the defence won't be totally sure which one is going to play the free kick. You might have a player with a strong shot in your team, and another who is very accurate with chips or crosses. Provided your players have been well briefed in set-piece play it's possible to fool the opposition by one of the players making a dummy run at the ball.

At Old Trafford we sometimes use three players in this type of move – Gordon Strachan, John Sivebaek and myself – and we have a number of variations as to who actually takes the kick.

I suppose the most used move from a set piece is the shot at goal by the 'secondary kicker', the player who lines up behind and to one side of the ball. The ball is rolled into his path for him to have a strike at goal from an angle 'round' the wall.

Playing the simple move well

By placing a strong, tall player in the opposition penalty area it's also possible to create a scoring chance even when it looks as if all the openings

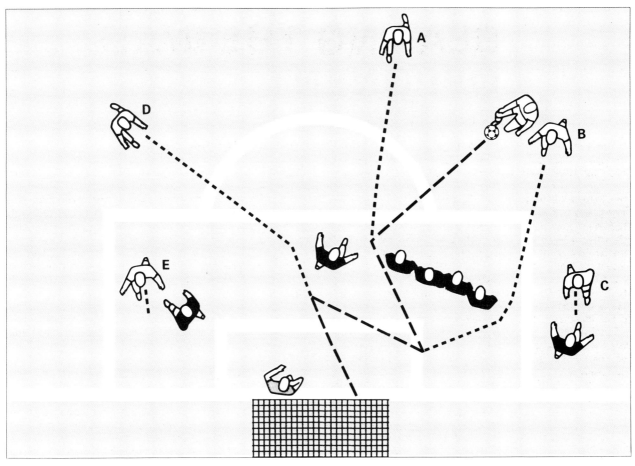

have been covered.

The idea is for the free kick to be aimed at this player so that he can knock the ball down to a player running in from a wider position. He'll have his back to goal when the kick is taken so the opposition will have a defender behind him, blocking his turn. Because of this it's more difficult for the defence to get at the ball and the attacker will be able to get his body in the path of the ball and volley, chest or head it towards a colleague.

He can also play a low pass to a runner coming in behind the wall if the ball is hit along the ground to him, and if the defence is expecting a high ball this will also give the attack the advantage.

I can't emphasize enough how important it is to try out set pieces in training, but the fewer players you involve in them the better. It's not much good if you make your set pieces so confusing that players forget what's expected of them. Also keep any signals used as simple as possible.

An easy system is for the taker of the free kick to signal his intent by raising an arm, or putting his foot on the ball as the wall forms, or maybe the signal can come from another player who isn't actually going to touch the ball but is lining up behind it. But don't try any fancy number calling . . . leave that to the Chicago Bears!

ROBSON'S TIPS

● *Complicated set pieces can easily lead to confusion. If too many players are involved something will go wrong. Keep it simple and try not to use too many players in each variation.*

● *Signalling is another thing which should be kept simple. A good method is for a player to make a 'dummy run' over the ball to indicate a particular set piece, and for a variation on the theme another player could make the same run.*

● *A runner coming from 'behind' a free kick will always provide a problem for the defence. They can't mark him because they are covering their penalty area, and even if he doesn't touch the ball he could pull a defender out of position.*

A way round the wall: **A** has run at the wall as the kick is taken. He controls the ball and plays it behind the wall as **B** runs behind the defence. Attacker **D** comes in to meet his pass as **C** and **E** go on decoy runs to the left and right to pull defenders out of the wall.

▬ ▬ Path of ball
▪▪▪▪ Path of player

BEATING YOUR OPPONENT

❛ You can't play soccer standing still. You've got to keep moving around the field. When you're attacking you have to create space; when defending you close space down. And you do all this by movement ❜

We've all played games which have involved chasing a pal around the school field or the playground. Games like 'tag', where the object is to get away from the person who is 'it' before he can touch you, are centuries old.

In that game we would dodge about, weaving and changing direction to stop the tagger from reaching his goal. Well, in soccer we do the same, but the player we're trying to lose is our marker – the one who's trying to prevent you from getting to the ball or creating a space for a colleague to pass to you.

I think that the game of tag is the best example I can use because of the tricks you have to get up to in an effort to shake off a close marker. He'll watch your every move, and at the top level in soccer this means that he won't be 'ball watching' very often, if at all; he'll be watching you.

Losing your marker

When I've played in mainland Europe, either in a European club game or for England, I've played against sides who use the man-to-man marking system. You almost become related to the marker by the time the final whistle goes. He'll follow you everywhere – and it's up to you to try to shake him off.

One of the tricks I use to get rid of any marker who is close to me is not to make one run to get into space but a couple, or as many as it takes to lose him.

'Making a run' is the term used for setting off in

a direction which looks as if you are getting into position to receive a pass, but to shake off my marker I may have to spin round and run again in a different direction, leaving him still running in the original line. I have broken away from him, just like that game of tag, and now for a second I'm free to pick up a pass.

The game of soccer is all about movement. Running off the ball is so essential that I should be telling you this in letters ten feet tall rather than through the words of a normal printed page.

Don't stand still

If a team-mate has the ball don't stand and watch him: get yourself moving into a position where he can pass to you, or set off on a run which will pull a defender out to mark you. If you know that a team-mate will be backing up and ready to take the pass then run out wide, draw the defender and let the pass go to a colleague. Even then your job isn't over, because you have to get back inside to help out again. It's a non-stop game. No standing still!

In the previous section I mentioned the zonal marking used a lot in the English game. This means that a defender is going to cover his zone, and mark any player in it, but he will also move over to help out the defender who's alongside him. If as an attacker you can get one of these defenders away from his zone, and leave a gap for a run through from midfield by a team-mate, then you'll have done the job of beating your opponent without even touching the ball.

Right: Losing your marker is essential if you hope to create an opening. I'm trying to join in an attack but I'm well covered.

Centre right: I feint to run to the marker's right but as my opponent transfers his weight to his right foot I change direction.

Far right: The body swerve without a ball has given me the opening I wanted. The marker will have to turn to chase, but I'm clear to run down the opponent's left side.

Remember that it's no use making every run a 'dummy' or the defence will realize that all you're doing is trying to pull one of them away and not take part in the move, and they will leave you alone. It's all a matter of trying to outwit your opponents, and the clever player will always be one step ahead of his marker.

One trick that's used by top players is to run into a wide position, drawing the defender, then spin and go back into the move rather than acting as a decoy. This means that you can never be left alone, and if you're always a worry to the defence then you've already got the advantage.

One of the best examples of this type of player that I can think of is Gary Lineker. He'll convince the defender that he's going to run into a space to pick up a pass, but just as the ball is about to be played will spin round and run in behind the marker who's still going towards the original space. Gary is then behind his man, who's trying to turn, and if the ball is then played through or chipped over the defence nobody will catch a player of Lineker's speed and control.

Acceleration is the key

Beating your opponent needs speed, but equally important is acceleration over a short distance. Nobody could beat Denis Law over five or ten yards; they might well catch him over 100 yards, but not in those first few vital steps. Diego Maradona is another who has tremendous control when he's on the ball, and amazing speed off it. He can shake off his marker by just running faster than him, and that's why players with this sort of ability reach the top.

There are many ways of beating your opponent. You can outwit him, outpace him and trick him with good ball control. But you must always be aware that he's also trying to deceive you.

You have to be on your toes in more ways than one. So no standing around and certainly no day-dreaming!

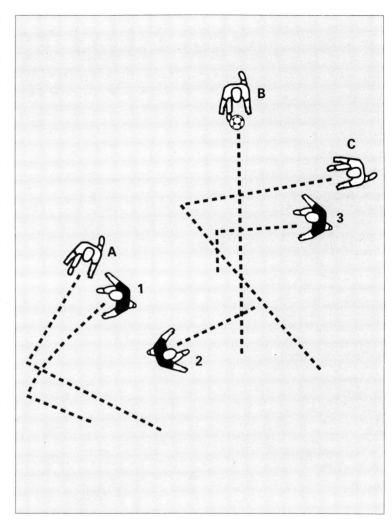

ROBSON'S TIPS

● *Never stand still. Always keep moving into a new position where you can either take on a pass or draw an opponent out of position.*

● *Running into a false position can drag a defender into an area where he doesn't want to go, but the player on the ball must be able to read the situation or the dummy run can be wasted.*

● *The one-two pass can take you through defences without a man-to-man challenge. It needs accurate passing and good running into space by those involved and there must be back-up support in case it breaks down.*

● *Practise spins and twists to change direction: these help you to 'lose your marker'.*

A and C draw defenders away from B, who holds the ball and runs forward. A runs to the right to draw with him a defender, turning inside to try to lose his marker. Attacker C cuts behind B to pick up a pass and attracts defender 2 to cover as well as his marker 3. This decoy run leaves the way open for B who has the alternative of passing to either colleague.

▬ ▬ ▬ ▬ Path of player

BEATING THE SYSTEM

❛ I'd rather play against the 4-3-3 system (the most popular in the English domestic game) than any other. The reason is simple: it gives the fans attractive soccer to watch. It can be very frustrating watching a game where the opposition play to a system that's so defensive and hard to crack. No doubt someone will come up with an idea soon that will revolutionize things once again . . . then there'll be yet another system to beat it **❜**

Right: Anticipation leads to a chance to score. A high ball is played into the penalty area and even though the defence appears to have the goal well covered the attack has a player coming in from the right.

Below right: The knock down isn't picked up by the defence and by anticipating the move I can beat the system. Had I attacked the ball I wouldn't have been in a position to score.

Throughout this section of the book we've looked at the various tactics you can use to attack and defend in certain positions and situations. Before moving on to another vital aspect of your game, I'd like to look for a moment at how to beat the system: what to do when the opposition plays to a particular pattern.

The sweeper When you're playing against a side that uses a sweeper you must try to switch play as often as possible. One of the mistakes that teams usually make if they face a sweeper is to try to break through the opposition's defence along the same channel time and time again. But this is playing into the hands of the sweeper who hasn't a lot to do; he just waits for the moment when the ball comes free from one of the defence and mops it up.

By switching play and trying to turn defenders the attack can give the sweeper problems. He can't be in two places at once, so if you can pull the defence over to one side, then turn just one of the markers and change direction to the opposite flank, you'll create an opening.

The aim of the attacking strikers must be to get

behind the central defenders, turn and lay the ball off to one side or the other. The sweeper will be able to cover only one area, leaving the midfield men space to get through.

Essentially it needs a good strong run from a forward to get into the defence and swift backing up from other members of the attacking side to get into the space he creates.

4-2-4 and 4-3-3 These are the most familiar approaches to the modern game in England. The secret of breaking down such systems is good backing up in the defence. You need strong players in wide positions and a defence that's disciplined enough to have players moving across to cover.

If the opposition attacks down the flank the midfield defender must back up the challenge of the full-back and always have support coming in from behind him. They only way to counteract the modern systems is to have a mobile defence so that it's not simply left to man-against-man play.

4-4-2 This is probably the hardest orthodox system to crack. Because there are eight players in defence it's always difficult to get openings in the

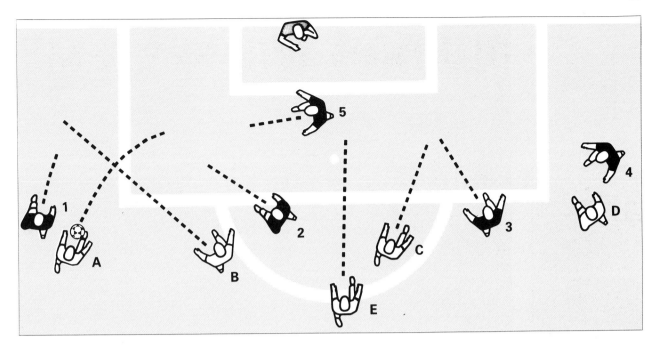

target area. To play it needs midfielders who get through a lot of work, since they have to help out the attack and then get back to defend. To beat it needs patience and pressure, and this is where individual skills can come out on top.

As I've said before, if a team comes to defend you have a lot on your hands, but there's always a way round if you work hard enough.

The unorthodox approach Some top level sides have adapted styles of their own. I've mentioned Sheffield Wednesday and Watford earlier, and their approach is unique. They look for balls being knocked down by their big forwards, and play to the strength of having tall players up front who are good in the air. The ball is often played to them from fairly deep positions, cutting out a lot of the build-up play in midfield, and the tall players head down to runners coming through 10 or 15 yards from them.

To counteract this the defending side must put players on the runners who are coming through, because that's where the real danger is going to come from. The defensive midfield have got to get in behind the strikers so that they can anticipate where the ball might drop as their strong players challenge.

The attacking goalkeeper A lot of goalkeepers today are finding time to leave their penalty areas and help out the back four. It's something which has caught on since we have seen some of the more extrovert antics of World Cup keepers, but it can certainly work if approached sensibly.

It's no good a keeper running up to tackle on the halfway line, but he can 'sweep up' just outside his area when there's room for him to do so, without causing any defensive problems.

Goalkeepers are usually good long kickers, and if they take free kicks in their own half of the field

Beating the sweeper system: Here **E** is the key attacker. **A** carries the ball inside, pulling his marker **1** with him. Attacker **B** runs behind him into a wide position and draws defender **2**. Attacker **C** runs to the right followed by defender **3**, which could bring attacker **D** into the move if the ball is played to the right and defender **4** has to cover this possibility. The sweeper **5** has to decide on his best position and moves over to cover the pass from **A** to **B** which seems the most obvious, but this leaves an opening for **E** to run through the centre to pick up the ball from **A**.

▬ ▬ Path of ball
▬▬▬▬ Path of player

they can give their attack the advantage by having one player more than normal in the opposing box.

But be careful: the time will come when the keeper miskicks. He will be well out of his goal area and if the opposition wins control he might have the embarrassing job of having to race back 40 or 50 yards as the ball sails through the air and into his net.

SUPPORT PLAY

❝ Some of the game's most outstanding modern players are those who don't fit into a particular category. The best support players are those who always seem to be involved either when their side is on the attack or when it's under pressure. Perhaps they should wear more than one number on their shirt ❞

One of the most important roles you can play during a game is simply that of the player who's always there! That may sound a little odd, but being in the right place at the right time is so vital to successful soccer that I feel I've got to single out the skill of supporting play.

I've mentioned it many times already, but soccer is not a game of standing still waiting for something to happen close to you. It's vital, especially for young players, to realize the importance of backing up a colleague and getting into positions where you can help out or continue the movement.

You may feel that this 'invisible player' isn't really fulfilling an important role, but when I say that this is the sort of job that I feel Kenny Dalglish and Diego Maradona do, then you will see how crucial it is.

Supporting play is the job of every player on the field. He needn't be a midfielder who comes back to help his defence, or a full-back who likes to have a sprint down the wing. He must be both of them and more besides!

In an attack it's up to the players on the side of the pitch where the movement begins to get involved.

The 'invisible player'

In the same way that defenders play 'off' each other, so the supporting players in an attack must be there to make things work. If the attack is down the right flank, then not only does the right winger move downfield, but also his colleagues on that side of the field should do too.

The right-sided midfield player should be alongside him looking for the pass, while the right full-back should be behind him in the attack and not standing on the halfway line watching play. This turns a one-man move into a three-man attack.

Support should also come from other areas. The right-sided central defender should go into a position to cover the breakout by the defence, taking himself into the full-back's zone but up over the halfway line, and the rest of the players should also move across to look for openings.

Things will be happening all the time during any part of an attacking move or a defensive

1 A perfect example of support play. A colleague has the ball and is approaching the opposition box. I begin a blind run behind him.

2 Will I pick up the pass? That's the problem for the defence who decide to cover my run.

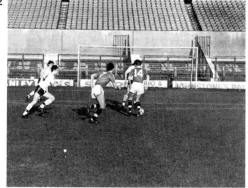

5 The attacker runs left as I run right pulling two defenders with me.

6 The defender covering the attacker on the ball realizes that I'm going down the left and turns to chase. The two other defenders are still chasing me.

counter, but whoever has the ball needs support just as much as the player making a challenge must have a colleague covering behind him to pick up the loose ball.

So the 'invisible player' is the one who is always getting himself involved in the action. He can create chances, score goals and stop the opposition from breaking through. Soccer should never be a game of 'that was your job not mine': it's very much a team game and being part of a team means supporting the play all the time.

Supporting the man on the ball: **A** carries the ball forward as colleagues **B** and **C** offer several alternatives by thoughtful running. Moves marked **1** are runs into space which would be to pick up a pass, run **2** is another supporting position to link up play, while **3** is a decoy run to draw a defender and allow the move to continue. A successful move would involve **A** linking with **B** or **C** while the free man draws an opponent away from the play.

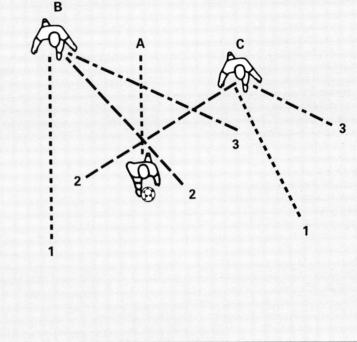

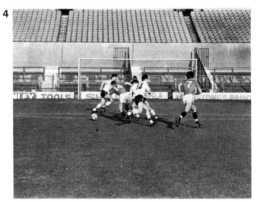

3 The defender challenges the player on the ball as I continue my run to the right. My marker and the covering centre-back move with me.

4 The challenging player sees me and hesitates. This opens a way down the left.

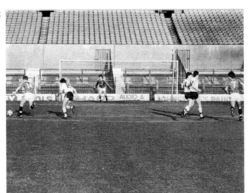

7 There is still a chance that the ball could be played to me so the cover continues but the player on the ball is now clear.

8 By drawing the two defenders to cover my run I've created a scoring chance for my colleague

PLAYING SWEEPER

❛I think because of the English weather and the number of games played during a season, players don't have the time to develop overall skills. If it's very wet and muddy you can't play the same type of game as you can in a warm dry climate, so skills suffer. And while there are probably just as many talented players in England as in any other country they don't get the opportunity to use those skills. That's why I think that the sweeper system has never been adopted – it needs a special sort of player ❜

The sweeper is a rare sight in the English game, but some of the top clubs have introduced this style of play, especially those who have been involved in European competitions.

It's a method of tightening your defence by having a free player operating behind the back four. This 'libero' was the secret of the defensive style introduced by the Italians in the 1960s, and it is a tactic which makes it very difficult for the opposition to score.

How it works is basically simple, although a lot depends on the talent of the person playing sweeper.

The back four are responsible for marking the four attacking players on the opposition, while the sweeper covers behind them. If a back-four player has to challenge for the ball the sweeper will play off him and 'pick up the crumbs'. If the four have marked up tightly the sweeper has the chance of intercepting a pass and, as the free player, can start an attack for his own side.

Essential qualifications required by a good sweeper are an ability to read the game, to anticipate the next move and, as well as all round ball skills, to be able to talk to his back four and make sure that they are always in the right positions.

That's why you often find that the side is captained by the sweeper whenever a team plays to this style.

A demanding role

It isn't an easy position to play because while a sweeper might not have a lot to do when his side is attacking, when they are defending he's responsible for covering everyone in the back four. He can do this only by weighing up the opposition and placing himself in an area of the pitch where he's closest to both the current move *and* the next possible switch in play.

If the attack turns one of his defenders he's got to get in and take over from that player until he's recovered his position. The nearest thing to compare with the sweeper style of play in the normal English game is the role of the 'spare' full-back when the opposition is playing 4-3-3.

Because they don't attack with two wide players the full-back who isn't marking up the winger (there's only one wide player and he's on the opposite flank) must cover his back four colleagues as they close down the attack. That's one player covering three, but the sweeper has to cover the whole of the defensive quartet and has to be very mobile.

The sweeper is going to have a lot of the ball, so it is important that he can create openings as well as closing down opponents. When he's picked up off the back four his role is to go forward looking for support from midfield and the attack, so he also needs pace and endurance.

At the start of a game the sweeper will line up about 10 or 15 yards behind the rest of the defence, usually in the centre of the field; in front of him will be the back four, usually three men in midfield and two strikers, but this is flexible, a 1-4-3-2 formation.

I've seen sides relying on just one striker, but that's usually when they're defending a lead in a European game or trying to keep the score down so that they can take advantage of the home leg.

One good reason for using the sweeper system is to upset the opposition. If you find that the style of a particular side does not suit the defensive tactic of using the sweeper it can be to your advantage to try it out.

Liverpool experimented with it in the early days of Kenny Dalglish's management, and other clubs used it when they needed to stop the opposition from scoring. Manchester City under Billy McNeill switched to using a sweeper, and for a time it worked.

But one of the problems tacticians face in England is that player are so used to playing to the normal system of just four defenders across the park, that the switch to using a sweeper can cause confusion.

Spare player in defence – and in attack

However I've got to stress that playing with a sweeper isn't just a defensive tactic. When the sweeper comes forward with the ball he's a very dangerous threat to the opponents. Players aren't prepared for long runs from deep positions and they will have picked up players closer to them, expecting the ball to be played in that direction. But if the sweeper pushes through he then becomes not the free player in defence but the attacking libero!

I've played sweeper for England on several occasions and I've got to admit that I really enjoyed it. I suppose it's because I've always liked being really involved in a game. I like to be on the ball as much as possible and getting where the action is, and as the sweeper I could do this and I didn't have the worry about not looking after a particular player in a certain area.

Reading the game

There's no doubt that I got some satisfaction out of linking up with the midfield and the attack, but I also found that playing sweeper gave me the chance to read situations much better when we were defending.

You can see the game from a distance, watch as your back four partners close down a move and decide where you are going next to make the best of things.

I've also got to emphasize that the sweeper isn't going to have it all his own way during a match. The back four may have marked up the attack, but the opposition midfielders are also going to penetrate so there are times when the sweeper is marking a player just like anyone else. But he plays his most effective role when he's tucking in behind to get the loose ball and set things moving forward again.

Changing styles

Foreign players coming into the British game have sometimes taken time to adjust because they have been forced to play with a different set of instructions from British players.

One of the best examples I can think of is John Sivebaek, my Manchester United team-mate, who came from Danish soccer. Now many players have come into the game from abroad, but not too many full-backs, and especially those who for most of their careers have played with a sweeper supporting them.

John suddenly found himself plunged into a game where he wasn't man-to-man marking but was covering a zone, and even though he was a top international he found it difficult to play to the English style. He had to tackle his wide player, push him away from the middle of the field, then get back and chase into the corner to cover. He couldn't believe it if a winger got past him and there was no sweeper coming in to whip the ball away after John had done the job of unbalancing the player on the ball!

He would also stick to marking the opposition's wide player when the action was over the other side of the field, covering the area he was responsible for but from where there was no threat.

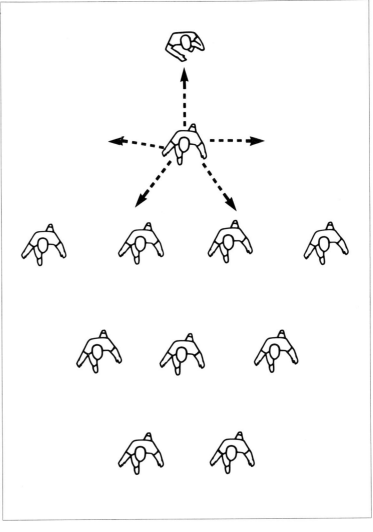

The sweeper plays behind the back four offering an alternative to zonal cover. He moves into space behind a colleague who is about to challenge or will link up in a forward move. The sweeper system works best with man-to-man marking in the defence with the sweeper free to pick up in defence or break forward in attack.

PLAYING CENTRAL DEFENCE

❝ I really admire a centre-back who can come away with the ball in the challenge and create an attacking move by carrying it forward under close control. There's no reason for a central defender to be a big, heavy-footed man. He should have height, the ability to get up above strikers and the foresight to read the next move – and if he's got strength and speed too he's well on the way **❞**

Top of the priority list for a central defender has got to be stopping the opposition from scoring goals. That may sound obvious, but it's something that coaches sometimes have to drill into would-be defenders who fail to understand basics.

Anyone playing at the centre of the defence should be taught to 'keep it simple' and 'keep it away'. There's nothing worse for a coach than to see his central defenders suddenly getting the urge to demonstrate their ball-playing skills when the opposing forwards are bearing down on them. It's at times like that the strong men at the back should stick to the simple things in life and get the ball away from the danger zone.

Central defenders – they were 'centre-halves' at one time – are tall, strong players, good in the air and powerful enough to hold off the threat that comes from the opposition's front players. But they must also be good readers of the game, able to see what's likely to happen in the next move and take steps to cut out the problems.

Keeping goal-side

Once again I should mention the defender's golden rule: never let the forward get goal-side of you unless you're trying to play him offside. If you do, you're in trouble!

I suppose that one of the most important aspects of the central defender's game is timing – more so than most other positions because he's in an area where mistakes can count. He has to time his jumps at the ball, either from lofted drives downfield, or to clear away threats from a corner, and he has to make sure that he tackles firmly but fairly in and around the box.

I say fairly because while some players can take risks with tackles in midfield or up in the opposition's half, because of the position the central defender finds himself in, to mistime a challenge can lead to a dangerous free kick, or even a penalty.

So he's a strong man, a player who can jump well, and not only must he be good in the air but he must also have confidence in the tackle and be powerful enough to hold off any challenge. Not bad credentials for a position that's not quite as glamorous as some.

Twin tasks

Most teams play with twin centre-backs nowadays, one left and one right, and both working off one another as well as their appropriate full-back. So the central defender is not alone in the back

four; if he makes a mistake he can rely on support from either side. But he has also to remember that he has to back up the players to his left and right.

The central defender should always try to be positioned so that when his 'twin' is challenging, he is about 10 or 15 yards off him, supporting the tackle and covering any run which might be made by another of the forwards.

The two defenders in the middle are there to stop any forwards having a clear run at goal and they have to work together to make sure that this doesn't happen. They work in pairs usually – one going for the player with the ball, the other covering him.

But any centre-back should always be aware that his place is in the middle of the defence, not simply on the heels of a centre-forward, or he will pull you out of position and leave a big hole for his colleagues to exploit.

Good pace is a valuable asset for any player and in a central defender it is an added bonus. Two great examples of this are Everton's Kevin Ratcliffe and our own Paul McGrath. Both are tall strong players but they are very quick, even though their size might make them look a little slower than the shorter players around them.

Dangerous positions

Because they have the pace they can often risk going forward and getting in what we call false positions because they have the speed to get back if anything goes wrong.

Losing possession can be a nightmare for a

central defender, simply because of the area in which he mainly operates. If he gives the ball away outside the penalty area you can more or less guarantee that the opposition is going to have a shot at goal, so he should get rid of any ideas of being too creative under pressure.

If a ball comes bouncing awkwardly towards him on the edge of the box the central defender will earn little applause from the crowd, and certainly no praise from the coach's bench, if he tries to do pretty things with it. If he's under pressure the centre-back must remember to stick to the simple things, even if that means belting the ball upfield as far as he can!

It may not sound very constructive, but it usually works, and you don't find many forwards scoring if the ball is back in their half of the field.

Centre-backs in attack

However I must say that I admire players like Liverpool's Alan Hansen, who not only tries to win the ball from advancing forwards, but also keeps possession. He can challenge, come up with the ball and then start an attacking move from his own half because he has good control and vision. He will move forward into space and lay off an accurate pass rather than just boom the ball upfield, and his style is one for any young player to emulate.

Young centre-backs have got to learn the dividing line which tells them when they should try to move upfield holding the ball and when it's perhaps wiser to get it as far away as possible. That lesson comes through practice and through the development of their skill to read the game.

Set-piece roles

A centre-back can also move upfield for corners and free kicks, and his height and strength are of great value. The tall man on the near-post for a corner is a familiar sight, and many scoring opportunities have been set up by using this tactic.

Tall centre-backs can use another trick when they join the attack, and that's to position themselves on the goal-line between the posts in front of the goalkeeper. Jack Charlton did this during his playing days and the idea rubbed off on Gordon McQueen who followed in his footsteps at Leeds before moving to United. They were both well over six feet tall and by putting themselves in that position they unsighted the keeper. It wasn't a dirty trick: they simply used their height in a different way, and Jack even used to jump up and down while the corner was on its way to make things even worse for the poor goalie!

So the central defender need not to be looked on as a someone who plays in an unattractive position. He is crucial in defence, but he can also create play as well as cutting out danger, and if he has the speed there is nothing to stop him being very useful in attack. Luton's Steve Foster is a great example of an attacking centre-half, good in defence but from set pieces always a handful for the opposition's back four.

Far left: Playing central defender I'm under pressure at a corner. I outjump the attacking player to get to the ball first.

Centre left: Having reached the ball I've no alternative but to head it back out of play. All other areas are covered.

Left: The ball goes for a corner. Had I headed away from goal I would have risked giving the ball back to the opposition. Central defenders must always keep their game simple.

PLAYING FULL-BACK

' If you're a full-back your priority is to defend. Nowadays overlapping backs are seen in virtually every game, but the full-back is first and foremost a defender – and if he forgets this he isn't helping his team '

People often joke that full-backs are really frustrated wingers, but there's a lot truth in it. To play at full-back in today's game you have to have good control, be able to read the game well and most of all have speed.

If that sounds like the qualifications you would need to play out on the wing it's quite true. There is a similarity, but the full-back must also possess an ability to tackle and win the ball for his side.

The role of the full-back is clear cut: he is a defender. If the opposition is playing with a winger the full-back needs no other instructions than to go out and stop the winger from getting involved in the game. But if there's no wide player for him to mark the full-back of the modern game comes into his own. He has space, he has pace and the rest is up to him.

Defensive duties

But I'd better start by describing some of the defensive duties a full-back should fulfil. Left or right doesn't really matter – the roles are the same – but let's imagine that the opposition has a winger playing on the flank the full-back is covering.

He knows that during the game the attack will try to bring the winger into play as often as possible and he has to be in a position to cut out any passes played in that direction, to challenge whenever the winger does get hold of the ball and, most important, he must also be aware of what is going on around him.

At times the attack is going to put the winger out wide yet not use him in their move. The full-back has to decide whether he stays with him or helps out in defence, and he can do this only through experience.

He must be able to judge whether the opponent is in a position where he can effectively take part in the move, and get himself between the winger and the goal, keeping an eye on his opponent at all times.

If the full-back is playing against a side which perhaps uses two strikers and just one winger, in a 4-3-3, or 4-4-2 formation, his job is to work off the shoulder of his central defender – helping out whenever there is an attack, picking up the midfield men who may make a run-through, and watching out for runs by the opposition full-back down his flank.

The importance of covering

Covering is an important part of the full-back's role. He should always be in a position where he can prevent anyone making a straight run through the defence, covering the central defender if the attack is down the middle, and moving up to cover the attack when necessary.

Full-back is an interesting position. Gone are the days when they looked like ex-convicts from a comic strip ready to kick the winger over the grandstand roof. Today they are built more like midfield players, and if they have speed as well that's a great asset.

Keep off the posts

Although there may be examples when full-backs don't stick to their traditional duties, you'll usually find that when the opposition has a corner the full-back will place himself on the near post – so for a corner on the opposition's right the left-back takes the near post. A word of advice here: never lean on the post. I've seen young players actually leaning on an upright during a game, but leave that sort of thing to Rip Van Winkle!

What I do if I've played full-back is to touch the post with my fingers to gauge an arm's length and position myself on the goal-line. The idea behind this is to act as a second goalkeeper if the ball beats the real keeper from the cross. You hold your ground until the time to move out and act as protection for the keeper if he goes to attack the cross.

Even if the keeper stays on the line himself, the full-back should stay there too, or just in front of it, to act as extra support in case a shot comes in.

I can't think of the number of times I've seen a full-back clear the ball off the line, or head out a shot that would be a certain goal when he's positioned himself in this way for a corner, so experience speaks for itself!

Attacking full-backs

Modern tradition is for the full-back to join in the attack and some of today's playing patterns allow this. When the back finds himself without a wide player to mark he should always try to add width to his own team by moving up into an attacking position as a secondary winger. During a game the opposition strikers will probably try to prevent the ball from getting across to the wide full-back, but if he can get away his speed should be able to cause problems for the opponents.

John Sivebaek is the perfect example of the modern full-back. He has strength and speed, and when he plays against a side that offers no real challenge down its left flank, John likes nothing better than to race into the opposition half and use his pace.

What we look for is for John to play the ball off to a midfield player or a striker if he gets it on the right, and then for the next pass to be played up to John who has overlapped the defence. It's a way of introducing a second winger into your attack, and used by many teams nowadays.

England have Kenny Sansom in their left full-back position, and while he's nothing like the build of Sivebeak he's a highly competent back. He likes to get forward a lot, and he's a good dribbler who can take on an opponent just like any traditional winger would.

But those two examples of full-backs to watch are both at the top of their trade. If you play full-back you must remember that your main job is to defend, and that must be uppermost in your thoughts at all times. If you're a good defender then you're doing a good job for your team, but of course you should always be looking for the opportunity to attack.

I mentioned the role of the full-back when the opposition has been awarded a corner, but when the corner is for his side, or when there is a set piece play in the other half of the field, the full-back is the player who should be backing up. He should have the pace to get into positions where

---

ROBSON'S TIPS

● *A full-back must be mobile. He must back up the central defender when he challenges and the attack when it goes forward.*

● *If you're playing against a winger it's your job to make sure that he gets as little of the ball as possible, but interception can come only if you have read the move properly.*

● *Don't commit yourself to the challenge unless you have support.*

● *A full-back with pace is an asset to any side, because he can be used as an extra winger on the overlap.*

---

he can either attack or cut out the possible breakaway, and his tackling ability means that he's the ideal person to prevent the opposition from breaking out with the ball.

1 Playing full-back I go on the overlap with an attacking colleague.

2 By running down the flank I pull a defender wide to cover the danger.

3 The defender has two players to cover and is uncertain which way the ball will be played.

4 The overlapping full-back is a common ploy in the modern game and fast defenders can be a useful addition to an attack.

PLAYING MIDFIELD

❛ Midfield is the power-house of the side. The players who fill in the midfield have a great responsibility: if they get on top then their side will usually dominate, but if they fail to get control the opposition has the advantage ❜

As a ball breaks from the opposition defence the midfield man is ready to move onto it. Striker, defender, creator – that is the role of the midfield player.

The midfield player is association football's all-rounder. He's a player who can help out in defence, create from the centre of the field, and get involved in attacks just like a forward.

So midfield is no place for the slacker. It's a position which sees you on the move throughout the game, and I suppose that's why I enjoy playing there so much. Through different circumstances, I've played in various positions – but the one which gives me the most satisfaction is midfield.

For one thing you're always involved. It means that you have to be near the action. If the ball is back on your goal-line then you have to be supporting the defence; if it's down in the other half of the field then you should be trying to get into a scoring position, or laying on a pass to someone better placed than yourself.

Defender before attacker

I'd advise anyone just setting out on a career in soccer to make sure that they concentrate on getting their defensive qualities right in midfield. It's all right being able to burst forward and get the odd goal, but you'll be far more valuable to your side if they can rely on you in defence. Once you have confidence in your own half is the time to add to your credentials by building up your attacking ability.

If a team contains three, or at times, four competent midfield players they will be able to build a solid unit, provided they are mobile enough. When their defence is under pressure the midfield players have got to mark up, challenge and cover, and they are the ones who are expected to build attacks by bringing the ball forward. They are the playmakers.

I don't quite know why but there has been a sudden upsurge in the popularity of the midfield player. When I was a boy everyone wanted to be centre-forwards, getting among the goals, but now more or less every youngster that I speak to reckons he wants to play in midfield. Perhaps it's because they like to be in the action, or perhaps it's because they're just trying to impress me!

No, the midfielder is the all-rounder, and it doesn't surprise me at all that most young players want to play in midfield where they can be kept busy.

A range of qualities

Not everyone has the right qualities, of course. You have to be strong enough to challenge and fast enough to beat defenders; you have to possess a creative touch and be able to see openings as well as close down the opposition's moves; and I think you should also be able to get forward and score goals. Nothing gives me greater satisfaction than scoring, and after all that's the idea behind the game.

The midfielder's role may differ from player to player. Perhaps it would help if I singled out some examples and the styles of play they were or are famous for.

One of the greatest playmakers I've ever seen was Johnny Giles, who began his career with Manchester United in the 1960s and moved to Leeds during their great years. He had an amazing ability to pass the ball accurately and into spaces where he knew it could threaten the opposition. He could kick with both feet over any distance and this is a skill which I would always try to acquire.

Another is Kenny Dalglish, and although some people would say that he is a striker I would argue that his style is more that of an attacking midfielder. Kenny would start off in the attack but then lay off into the middle of the park and spray passes about, reading moves all the time and then going back into the striking line at the right moment.

An array of options

It's hard to talk about midfield tactics. There are so many ways of approaching the position that actual tactics may not come into it, but mobility certainly does.

ROBSON'S TIPS

● *Fitness is an essential quality of any midfield player. He has to cover a great deal of the field during any game, and must have the stamina to do so.*

● *A quick-thinking midfield player should be able to see an opening from almost any situation. He must always be looking for a way through the opposing defence.*

● *Midfield players have the responsibility of dictating play – but they must also work as part of the team and not as an individual unit.*

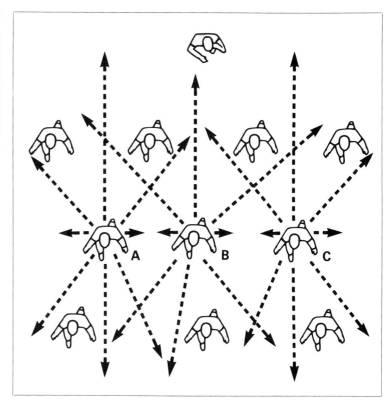

If we imagine an attack has just broken down in your half of the field and the ball has been won by your full-back, the midfield player on his side has to support him to get the ball forward. He can either act as a wall for a one-two pass, or carry the ball forward himself, but he too needs support.

This comes from midfield colleagues, one running wide and the other trying to draw a player away, leaving an opening through to the forwards. The midfielder with the ball has several choices – he can play to the wide player, or into the space created by the one who has drawn the defender, or play a long ball out to the far side of the attack, or find the forward closest to him and then run on to receive a return, or keep running. Such is the demand on the midfielder that if the move then breaks down he has to get back to win the ball again.

I like to get forward and I like to get into the opposition's box, where I might grab a goal. But I also like to get on the ball as much as I can so that I can start the passing movements going upfield. But if you compare my style of play with my pal Ray Wilkins' you will see another contrast in midfield styles.

He likes to dictate play from as early in the move as possible, even from the moment when the goalkeeper throws the ball out. Ray wants to be as far back as that and spray the passes about, getting himself into supporting positions behind the ball and shouting and directing things. It's a different approach from my own but in its own way very effective and valuable.

Playing wide midfield
Playing midfield can also mean playing wide almost like a winger but with other responsibilities. These players have to work really hard in my opinion, not only attacking down the flanks but playing the role of a ball winner in their own half, as well as supporting the full-back.

If anyone wanted an example of the style to adopt when playing as a wide midfielder I would single out Steve Coppell as one of the most outstanding exponents of this type of game. He

was a player who could fill an orthodox winger's shirt for part of the game and yet would battle for the ball in his own half with the tenacity of any top defender. Trevor Steven of Everton is in a similar mould.

So if you're one of the many midfielders hoping to make it to the top there's probably someone in the game whose style you'd like to emulate. If there is, study him closely and you'll see that he's mastered all the basic skills to perfection, added fitness to give him the pace and endurance which he needs, and that, most of all, he's a player who loves to be involved.

The midfield player should be prepared to cover every area of the field. At times he will have to run back to cover in defence, out wide to assist his full-back and forward to link up with the strikers. His role is to win back the ball in the centre of the field and to try to dictate play by creating openings for his attack.

The midfield player covers in defence. As his full-back challenges I'm ready to help out. The midfield player must be as willing to defend as he is to attack.

PLAYING WIDE

❝ Any young player filling a wide role, whether in midfield or on the wing, has got to be ready for hard work. He's going to fetch and carry the ball as the midfielder, and run at the defence time and again as the winger, and he can be ready for this type of challenge only if he's reached a high standard of fitness ❞

There are two clear areas of the game which can be described as playing wide. One is the role of the orthodox winger who takes up a position on the flank and whose main role is to take on the full-back and supply crosses to the central strikers, and the other is the outside midfielder in a 4-4-2 formation.

During my days with West Bromwich Albion I played a wide midfield role, but I have to say that I wasn't too happy there, because I really like to get more involved in the action.

One of the gifts a wide player must possess is patience, and that applies both to the winger and the wide midfielder. There can be times when you can go five minutes of a game and not get a decent touch of the ball – and that sort of thing certainly doesn't appeal to me!

But I would stress the importance of players who can play in wide positions and be extremely effective. Two who spring to mind are Arnold Muhren and Kevin Sheedy, contrasting players as far as style is concerned but equally proficient. When Arnold was with United he really impressed me with the way that he could wait for the right opportunity and then create something after apparently being out of the game for a few minutes. However neither he nor Kevin will stand around watching the rest of the players; they're always mobile and waiting for the right chance.

Working off one full-back, beating another

As we have seen, the wide midfield man is the link between the back four and the forwards just as the central midfielder is, but he works 'off' the full-back rather than the central defenders and can form a good working partnership on the flank.

Many teams have developed attacking styles which incorporate overlapping moves involving the wide midfielder and the full-back interchanging passes and challenging deep into the opposing half, with one or other cutting inside to form the link to the strikers.

And the roles are often reversed when the full-back is under pressure. He will then expect support from his wide midfielder dropping back to cover and collect.

Orthodox wingers are slightly different in that they are usually players whose skill is to carry the ball down the flank using speed and control and beat the full-back. When a side uses such a player I think that it's important that they get the ball to him as often as possible. The more that he gets involved in play the better opportunity his side will have of putting pressure on the opposition's full-back. Even if that full-back is not beaten, this can pull other defenders back to cover, leaving useful openings.

Right: The wide midfield player of the modern game is expected to help out his full-back in defence; here he supports a challenge.

Centre right: Picking up the ball after his colleague's tackle, the wide midfield player starts a run upfield.

Far right: He now has support from his full-back and the two players link to break forward.

Pace and control

To be a winger today you must have good pace and acceleration, since full-backs themselves are so fast now. The other areas you must be strong in are ball control, to beat a player with skill, and the ability (and strength in the case of youngsters) to cross the ball at speed.

There's nothing to stop a side having both a wide midfield player and an orthodox winger, and I can think of plenty who fit in this category. Here, if the winger switches flanks from time to time, he can create a three-player partnership on the wing: full-back, midfielder and winger can combine to raid the opposition and this is a successful way of creating chances.

Good 'dribblers'

The winger is usually the best dribbler in the side, and the wider the range of tricks he can have the better. He will be faced by defenders who want to make sure that the ball is on his 'wrong foot', to push wide when he tries to cut inside, or to let him run wide if he prefers to take the inner channel, so his ability to beat a player with good dribbling is very important.

In today's game the orthodox winger will not only be challenged by the full-back, but also by any opposing wide midfield player, so he has got to be able to pass accurately and see the opening knowing that he has pulled somebody into a wrong position.

One thing a winger does to the game is increase the entertainment level. In the past wingers have been the star attraction for some clubs, and one of the most famous was Stanley Matthews, who could fill a ground when the fans knew he was in town.

I've often been asked if a player like Stan could have survived in the modern game – and I'm sure

ROBSON'S TIPS

● *The wide midfield player must be prepared to support the full-back on his side whenever the opposition threatens.*

● *Wingers must have a wide variety of tricks. They cannot just rely on passing the man against them and trying to cross, but opening up other moves by good touches to inside positions.*

● *The full-back and wide player can form a good twin-strike force. Look for the opportunity to overlap and back each other up in the move – but make sure that you have cover from behind before over-committing yourself.*

he could. He was obviously very fit, and there's no doubting his ability. I'm sure he would have been just as big a star had he played in the 1980s rather than the years either side of the Second World War.

High work-rate

The biggest difference he would notice is that it's no longer just a case of beating the full-back and getting a cross in. Now the cover is so disciplined that there's always another defender backing up, and anyone who dwells on the ball is going to find himself under immense pressure.

The most outstanding wide player I've ever seen is George Best, and his style of play should be an example of the perfect player to anyone. He could take people on, pass the ball and get through a great deal of work during a game.

PLAYING STRIKER

❝ My number one striker is Ian Rush. I know that he and Gary Lineker score a similar number of goals, but Ian gets himself more involved in other areas of the game. He threatens defenders who stay too long on the ball and works for openings ❞

'Get out there and score some goals' should be the instruction given to every striker before a game, because that's precisely what his job is. He's the player who has to get himself into scoring positions, the target player the rest of the team will be looking for during attacking moves. The striker needs to be strong and fast and have both a powerful shot and the ability to get up to high crosses.

His role may not simply be to go for goal, however. Many clubs use their striker in a different way, and in some cases play with two contrasting players up front, working off each other.

The target players

One system is the target-player approach. The striker is the player that the others look for when they are starting an attack. The midfielders will work the ball forward and then pass to the striker, who's strong enough to withhold the challenge in the opponents' half while his midfielders move upfield. He then has to have the skill to work the ball to them as the attack develops.

It's a difficult game to play because most of the time you're the player upfield, usually with your back to goal and perhaps with support coming from only one colleague. You have to be able to control the ball, fend off the challenges and then find supporting players with a pass, before taking up a new position as the move continues. He is looking for an opening and hoping to get into the penalty area as the ball arrives to get a strike in.

The runner

The second familiar role of the striker is to make runs off a target player, playing off his support and hoping to get a shot at goal at the end of the move. Most clubs use two strikers, one filling each of the roles and the most successful clubs are those with players who have a good understanding of each other's play.

Ian Rush and Gary Lineker are perfect examples of players who can work off the target player. Neither gets too involved in the build-up play, but once the ball has been played on for them they will usually get a shot or header in.

They also illustrate another tactic used by strikers – running onto a ball knocked over the defence for them – because they have pace to get beyond defenders. This takes time to develop, for those distributing the ball have to know the correct position in which to play the pass, and the strikers have to be ready to move onto it.

Balance, courage and hard work

Strength isn't as important with a striker as it used to be, but balance certainly is – and courage. Because most of their game is spent sprinting into the opposing half they will take knocks from defenders who try to take them off the ball, so sure-footedness is essential.

The striker has to work hard when the opposition has the ball in its own half to worry them into making mistakes. And they have also got to challenge for high balls with the opposing centre-backs.

Andy Gray and Graeme Sharp are two players who fit into what I would call the old-fashioned centre-forward mould. They're great at winning the ball in the opposition box to lay it off for a supporting player. Mark Hughes is another who would physically fit into this bracket, but he liked to play off a target player, letting Frank Stapleton knock down for him to strike.

So any young player with aspirations of making it as a striker should see which of the basic roles he prefers to play and build his game up around this. If he likes to lay the ball off and is good playing with his back to goal then he will certainly find an opening in the game, and if he has the Rush or Lineker touch his future is secure!

ROBSON'S TIPS

● *Get into the box as often as possible; just the fact that you're there will be a threat to the defence. Try to 'feel' that you know where the target is without lifting your head when a chance arises.*

● *Remember that the knock-down to a well-placed team-mate is just as likely to produce a goal as the header at the target. Try to surprise the opposition by changing tactics.*

● *Jump across in front of defenders for high balls, because even if you fail to make contact you should put them off enough for your colleagues to win the advantage.*

● *Strikers running onto a cross should always try to approach goal from an angle, rather than square on. This gives you the advantage over a goalkeeper who has to leave his line to cover the far post.*

Left: The striker's job is to score goals. He has to be on the lookout constantly for an opening in the opposition's box. Here the ball breaks off a defender.

Centre left: The defence races to cover but the striker is clear.

Bottom left: He times his run with precision and prepares to shoot as the cover closes in.

FITNESS FOR SOCCER

" Boredom can lead people into things like smoking and taking drugs, but if you have soccer you can't be bored. The game gives you something to do all the time. Even when you get out of bed first thing in the morning you should exercise lightly "

Being fit and healthy must rate as highly in a would-be soccer player's list of priorities as skill itself. If you're not fit then you can't give your best on the field, and if you don't look after your health then you'll never be fit.

I know there is very little we can do to prevent us from catching a cold or going down with a bout of 'flu, but we can make sure that we are fit enough to fight off the symptoms as quickly as possible and get back on our feet again.

Say no to drugs

Young players can, however, avoid one of the enemies of football right from the start – and that's smoking.

Later in life alcohol joins in to make things hard if those around you over-indulge, but I know that while most top players enjoy a social drink after a game or on an evening out with their family and friends they all know about the problems smoking can cause.

I couldn't be more against smoking, and it's something which to me just has no point. It's a bad habit, just like some young lads get into things like flicking their hair back with a toss of the head and find they can't stop doing it. Smoking is very much the same except it's dangerous, dirty and expensive. If you get into it you can't stop without a lot of effort, so why start in the first place?

All I'd say to anyone who thinks that he can smoke and enjoy sport – and that of course means soccer – is that he has another think coming! If you want to smoke, just ask a smoker why he does it and if he'd like to stop. You'll find that most of them do it out of boredom and would love to give it up, but they haven't got the will power to succeed.

Another danger young people face nowadays comes from drugs. I know little about drugs – for me they're just something you read about in the paper or the doctor might prescribe if someone is ill. But I do know of their dangers, and there's no fun in even finding out about drugs. Leave them well alone if you want to be healthy.

Personal fitness is exactly what it sounds like; it's a personal responsibility, and it's up to you to make sure that you're fit enough to enjoy your sport.

In this section I'm going to look at the various ways you can bring yourself up to a certain standard of fitness for soccer, and one message that I must put across to anyone who intends to enjoy a game is that you can't cut corners. If you

want to be a soccer player it takes a lot of hard work. It's no good thinking that because you have ball skills they'll carry you through a game.

Skill will help you to play the game well, but fitness will help you to do it for 90 minutes.

Young players joining a professional club suddenly find themselves in another world. The standards of training are so much higher than they had been with their school side or their amateur club, and the demands made on them are that much greater, that they often wonder if they'll make the grade. Some, of course, do not.

Youngsters, and by that I mean anyone from say 7 to 13, need very little encouragement to run around and play soccer. The fact that they spend most of their time running anyway, whether it's down to the corner shop, home from school or around the playing field, means they have a lot of energy and so it isn't all that important. But building up *stamina* is.

Run for fun

As you get older running becomes more important. In fact the less you do it as part of everyday life the more you will notice that your energy goes when you do run. So older boys who only play soccer for fun should try to get in some exercise apart from the couple of nights' training they might put in with their club. Whether it's a club side, a pub side or just a group of pals who have formed a team, the fitter you are the more successful you will be and the more you will enjoy your game.

Jogging is ideal. A couple of miles each night will do you no harm. It'll build up your stamina, make your legs stronger and keep you fit for the next training session or fixture. After the run a short routine of simple exercises to tone down is a good idea. Work on stomach muscles and on strengthening your legs, because these are vital areas for the soccer player.

Morning routine

Loosening up exercises first thing in the morning are a good idea. Nothing drastic here – just good deep breathing to start with, filling the lungs with lots of air and then a little routine that involves touching the toes, stretching the thigh and calf muscles, some upper body loosening, arms on hips, legs apart bending to the side a few times and repeating with the opposite side of your body.

There's nothing wrong with that sort of loosener. It won't turn you into an international soccer player, but it won't do you any harm either, and if you feel good at the start of the day then you'll get more out of it.

One of the dangers for players who don't do anything except join in the training session twice a week is that they leave themselves wide open to injuries. It's very easy to pull a muscle even when you are fit – I certainly don't need any reminders about that – but when you're out of condition and plunge straight into an exercise you can quickly find out the hard way.

The full-time player trains every day of the week with the exception of perhaps Sunday, and even then he will do some form of exercise if only to loosen up. So a short daily work-out is very important.

Keep it clean

Personal hygiene must also rank high on your list of priorities. A player's body is his main asset so he needs to look after it, and simple things like cleanliness should never be overlooked.

If you want to be a soccer player you have to look after your feet. There's nothing worse than having great long toe-nails, which can only cause you pain as well as problems. Your feet should also be kept clean and that means changing your socks every day and washing properly.

I'm sure that some of the foot complaints people get are only through neglect and therefore if you look after your feet they'll pay you back in

the end.

You're playing mostly on grass and that means that if you get cut or grazed you are going to be in contact with the soil and that can be dangerous. If you are a keen player it's worth seeing your doctor and having an anti-tetanus injection so that if you do get any dirt near or in a cut it won't lead to anything serious.

Personal hygiene is really down to pride. If you have no pride at all then you will show it in your appearance. You may not make it as a soccer player, but there's nothing to stop you being clean, tidy and healthy if you try.

Below left: A simple stretching exercise – reaching down to the side with one arm then repeating on the opposite side.

Below right: Trunk bending for suppleness. Arms behind the head, legs apart, lean over as far as you can to each side.

BUILDING LEG STRENGTH

❝ Sets of short, simple exercises can really improve your leg strength quickly. All you have to do is work out a programme that you can stick to every day and try either to increase the number of repetitions or add a little more time to the exercise as you get stronger. It's surprising how soon you will show a vital improvement **❞**

Building your physical strength for soccer is very important, although it's essential that young players realize where to draw the line. We don't want them to finish up like weight-lifters or one of those who kicks sand in the face of the weakling on the beach. What we're aiming for in soccer is stamina and strength, especially in the parts of the body we use most in the game.

Area one has got to be the legs. There can be no doubt that every top player has strong legs, for if he hadn't he wouldn't be able to stay the pace of the modern game.

Part of general fitness is a medium-distance run. We're not looking for a marathon man, just someone who can manage to cover two or three miles without too much effort. That begins the strengthening process, and should be capped with a sprinting session to build extra strength into the thighs.

Routine exercise

There are many exercises to strengthen legs, and the first which springs to mind for me is the *squat thrust*. They're also a very good way to develop leg and body strength at the same time, although the emphasis is on the legs because they take most of the strain.

Start in a press-up position – that is, face down on the floor with legs together – and lift the upper body by pressing your hands and arms down at shoulder width. This puts your head in the air and creates an area of space between your arms and upper body. Supporting your weight on your arms you then spring forward with both feet so that you finish in a squat with your hands still flat on the floor. Then spring back again into the starting position, which is similar to the way you finish at the top of a press-up.

The idea is to repeat this exercise jumping forward into the squat, then thrusting the legs back to the start. Squat and thrust . . . the squat-thrust.

I've got to emphasize at this point that we're talking about preparing you to play soccer, and therefore exercises like the squat-thrust are aimed at strengthening certain areas of the body. It's not a competition to see how many times you can bring your feet up under your shoulders, or a race against time: it is an exercise.

Work on a simple routine. Start with 20 squat-thrusts, for example, and build on a few more every couple of days. Some boys will find that they can manage many more before they begin to feel tired, and if so increase the minimum number

and then add to that as you improve. Do not overdo it, though: if you feel very tired, stop and have a rest. On the other hand, you will have to push your body to new limits for it to meet the highest standards.

Don't skip the skipping

To build up calf muscles there can be no better exercise than skipping! If you can't borrow a skipping rope or a length of clothes line, don't worry. Just go through the skipping motions as if you were miming to someone. Keep bobbing up and down avoiding that imaginary rope and you'll soon find that your calf strength is growing.

Here again you can set yourself a target every day, adding to it as you get better and stronger.

You'll find with skipping that it's easier to go for time rather than the number of skips because you can do so many in a short time you'll lose count. Set youself a target of 30 seconds with a one-minute rest, then another 30 seconds followed by another rest, and repeat this until you begin to feel the pressure on your calf muscles.

You'll probably find that after three sets of skipping you will feel tired, but that next time you try it it won't be as bad. After a few days you can step up the time you skip and shorten the rest in between. There is nothing unusual in a fit person being able to skip non-stop for five minutes at a time.

Hopping glad

Hopping on the spot strengthens the ankle and it's a good exercise for any player because he puts a lot of pressure on his ankles during a game. There's nothing difficult about the hop: just lift one foot off the floor – perhaps holding onto the ankle as the leg is pulled up behind you, and then hopping on the spot on the other leg.

By changing legs after a number of hops we can add this exercise to our programme, once again increasing the quality as strength grows.

Step-up in fitness

Step-ups are another addition and this is the type of exercise anyone can do to increase leg power. All you need is a chair or a bench – but not the best furniture!

It's a fairly simple procedure. Start with the left leg, and from a standing position in front of the chair raise the foot onto the seat as if you were

Step-ups are the perfect way to build up leg strength without using expensive equipment. A small stool should be used to start with, then a taller object, such as a wooden chair, when muscle power has increased. Here I'm using two gymnasium benches placed on top of each other.

climbing stairs. Then step up onto the chair until you finish in a standing position on the seat. Next step down again, leading with the left leg, and return to the original stance. Repeat this using the left leg for about 20 sets and then switch to the right.

In our gymnasium at the Cliff training ground we have a piece of equipment you can make yourself and use for strengthening your ankles.

It looks a bit like an object you'd expect a circus juggler to take into the ring with him but it's very effective.

It is in two parts, one a flat piece of board strong enough to hold your weight and large enough to stand on with your feet slightly apart, and the other a rounded piece of wood like a thick broom handle and cut to the same size as the board.

All you do is place the rounded piece on the floor so that it points between your legs, then place the board on it and keep your balance by putting one foot on each side. It's tricky, but it works . . . and you can wobble your way to fitness!

Don't use anything which is too high or you'll put extra strain on your legs. You're looking for a bench or chair which is around knee height.

So there we have it – a neat little routine of leg exercises to work at. But remember, don't overdo it at first. Build up to a level that gives you a 20-minute or half-hour work-out by lengthening the time taken over each set. If, after a period, you discover that you can get through each pro-gramme without raising too much of a sweat, speed things up to get more in within the time limit.

ROBSON'S TIPS

● *When carrying out any exercise, however simple, make sure that you don't overdo it. You aren't going for world records – you're trying to build up strength. So start with a low target and add to it, not with a high one you can't achieve.*

● *Simply raising yourself from a normal standing position onto tip toe will strengthen the lower leg muscles. By stepping up and down onto an object the exercise can be improved, and the upper legs strengthened.*

● *Anyone who can do 100 squat-thrusts has achieved a fairly high standard of leg strength and physical fitness.*

● *Hopping strengthens ankles and skipping helps calf muscles; a combination of both using a skipping rope is one of the simplest leg routines to give quick results.*

BUILDING BODY STRENGTH

‘ The more stomach exercises you do the stronger a runner you will be. It's very important to a soccer player that he has speed off the mark and this is achieved by getting explosive strength which starts from the stomach area. So any good training routine should include exercises which strengthen the stomach ’

They say that the way to a man's heart is through his stomach, but this age-old expression would have to be altered to ring true from a soccer point of view. Part of the path to top soccer fitness does, however, lie in the stomach muscles.

This may surprise many of you, but it's from this area of the body that power is built for sprinting, and that strength comes for physical contact.

If you're able to develop strong stomach muscles – and once again I must stress that I mean from an athletic rather than a body-building point of view – then you'll find that you can also improve other areas of your body.

Anyone doubting the value of stomach muscle development should try a simple little test. With both feet firmly on the ground get ready to do a 'star-jump': you'll notice that the first thing that you do is to rise onto the ball of the foot, and then tense the stomach muscles to prepare for lift-off.

Now get ready for a quick sprint – and again the muscles in the stomach area are 'switched-on' before there's any movement. Even kicking a ball requires a 'pulling through' movement which starts with the body (the stomach muscles mainly) before bringing the leg into the action.

So upper body strength is very important.

Explosive running

I think I can safely say that most top runners – with perhaps the exception of those who specialize in long distances such as the marathon – include plenty of body-work in their training routine.

Certainly the 'explosive runners', those who cover short distances, need good body strength, and when their type of running is broken down it's exactly the kind used in soccer. From the gun they want to get off the blocks as quickly as possible, they have to cover the first 10 to 15 yards swiftly, and force their body forward. This is exactly what the soccer player does: from a fairly stationary position he has to turn and explode into a sprint to chase a ball, to get into space or to close down an opponent.

So the upper body must be developed from a general fitness point of view. Exercises which will help include press-ups, which build arm, shoulder and back muscles, to simple 'jack-knife' leg raises for stomach strength. They can be built into any training routine and the best way for any young players to start on them is the same way as with the leg exercises, in short sets of ten, increasing as the exercise becomes easier to complete.

A routine for you

I'm sorry if I give a fairly vague figure when dealing with how many repetitions should form the basis of a routine, but I can't give a number which applies to everyone, because everybody has different capabilities.

You may be able to complete 50 press-ups before you begin to feel tired, or maybe as few as five; it all depends on the level of natural fitness you have already reached, while size, weight and strength have all got to be taken into consideration.

The aim of the routine is to give you a programme of exercises which will help to develop your body for sport, and for football in particular. If you find that you are shattered after just five press-ups then stop and have a rest. You must never push your body too far; if you feel that you cannot possibly go on with a routine then you're overdoing it.

What you should try to achieve is a series of exercises which allow you to 'work out' all the areas of the body which need to be supple and strong for soccer. If the routine is completed with little effort, then it's not hard enough and should be increased. If on the other hand you have to give up after just two parts then you've over-estimated your ability and must then cut down.

Press-ups and sit-ups

The press-up is possibly the best known exercise after touching your toes and it is of great value to the soccer player and there are three types of press-up which can be incorporated into any routine. They revolve around the arm positions and vary in difficulty. The easiest involves a wide arm placement, and the hardest has the hands close together.

Lie face down on the floor with your hands placed flat, palms down at shoulder width, elbows tucked in along your sides. With the weight of your legs supported on the balls of your feet, push down with your hands and straighten your arms. The aim is to keep the body in as straight a line as possible, and one press-up is completed when you return to the lowered position – but without your body resting on the floor.

Normally press-ups are done with the hands around shoulder width, but they can be made slightly easier by widening the hand position, and more difficult by narrowing it, until the hands are almost touching below the chest.

These exercises will improve chest, arm, and shoulder strength as well as helping to develop the muscles in the back, all of which are important to a soccer player. To concentrate more on the stomach muscles raise both feet off the ground by using a stool or a bench, and carry out a series of press-ups.

Another simple exercise to develop stomach strength is to lie on your back, hands behind your head, and (while keeping both legs outstretched with heels firmly on the ground), pull yourself up into a sitting position. The sit-up uses mainly the stomach and thigh muscles and is a fairly straightforward exercise which can be added to any routine.

In the case of a press-up, if you find it very difficult to complete a reasonable number you can begin from a kneeling position, forcing the upper half of the body off the floor but leaving the knees and feet there.

The same rule applies to sit-ups. If you find them impossible with outstretched legs, then bend the knees, tucking the feet under a piece of heavy furniture.

Once you have started to reach a reasonable level of fitness, however, you should be able to carry out all these exercises normally.

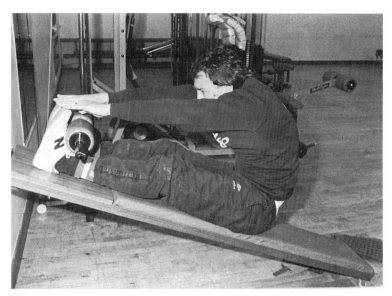

ROBSON'S TIPS

● *Exercises in sets of ten are perhaps the simplest way of building a routine. If you find it easier to do more do them, but don't overstrain any muscles or it will do more harm than good.*

● *A simple stomach exercise is to lie on the floor on your back, arms above your head, legs together. Rise to a sitting position and touch your toes as you lean forward, then return to the starting position slowly.*

● *Remember that the aim of exercise is to develop general fitness for soccer. You're not trying to compete for Mr Universe!*

Top right: Using a weight or solid object to support your feet, sit-up exercises strengthen both stomach and leg muscles. I'm using a specially-designed gymnasium bench which is set at an angle to increase the effect of the work-out. At home improvise by wedging your feet under a piece of furniture.

Centre right: Press-ups should be part of any work-out. Here my hands are close together to make the exercise more difficult.

Bottom right: This is almost yoga as I pull hard on my ankles lifting my trunk from the mat at the same time as I force my thighs off the ground. This strengthens legs, arms and shoulders as well as helping suppleness.

BUILDING CONFIDENCE

' As a professional soccer player I've had to learn to take the bumps and bruises of the game, and I suppose I can claim that I've had more than my fair share! But you need the confidence to take the physical side of the sport or you won't succeed as a player. Not all top players can be called 'physical', but they all know how to take a knock and don't let the threat of a heavy challenge put them off their game '

One area of soccer which can sometimes be the dividing line for a young player is the physical aspect of the game. It's very easy for a young player with a reasonable amount of skill to find that when it comes to the game itself he hasn't got the confidence required – or the nerve to get involved physically.

Now there's no way that you'll gain confidence for physical combat by reading the pages of a book, but I hope that I can pass on some advice which will help you overcome the problem if it is something which affects your game.

Bravery, toughness, playing hard, call it whatever you like – it's all part of the game of soccer. If a six-foot forward is running at you with the ball, you can't roll up into a ball and hope he'll go away; you have to challenge and this means that you must be confident in your ability.

Fair challenge
Most young players will only take part in games against players their own age, so they will be a similar height, weight and strength. In games like these there should be no reason to fear anyone.

You have the laws of the game to protect you from out-and-out dirty play, so provided you know how to make a challenge and carry it out fairly you won't get hurt – or hurt anyone else.

You'll get bumped and you'll get kicked. But you must learn to take the knocks, and always remember that the more confident you are in your own challenge the less likelihood there is of you getting hurt. If you pull away from a tackle your body will be in the wrong position and that's often how players pick up injuries.

When you get older you'll sometimes find yourself playing in open-age games where you may be faced with opponents who are fully matured while you are perhaps still a teenager. That's when your confidence in your ability and physical qualities come into its own.

In lower grades of soccer at open age younger players are on average much fitter than older members of the side, so fear comes in to play. Older players may try to scare youngsters with a strong challenge early in the game, or even with verbal threats. But you have to ignore that sort of thing, and show your opponents that you're a

Right: Withstanding a challenge is a way of building up confidence. I transfer my weight to my right side as a colleague tackles.

Far right: I switch the ball to my left foot, keeping it as far away as possible from the tackle, still fending off the challenge.

95

ROBSON'S TIPS

● If you pull away from a challenge, or only make a half-hearted tackle, you take a bigger risk of getting hurt than if you commit yourself totally.

● When holding off a challenger you must strengthen the side of your body closest to him by tensing the muscles in shoulder, arm, hip and thigh and have your non-contact foot firmly on the ground.

● A shoulder-charge – shoulder-to-shoulder contact – is meant to knock the opponent off-balance. When carried out within the rules, it's a fair way of using physical strength to your advantage.

player who doesn't run away from the action.

I must emphasize the importance of a player's confidence as well as ability to take a knock. If you cannot take the physical side of soccer you'll never make the professional game, and there's every chance that you'll struggle at amateur level as well.

You have to be strong enough in your mind to take the bumps and bruises and if you don't have this kind of strength then you won't be able to face the game physically.

'Steal ball'

I'm not trying to turn every reader into a toughie – just pointing out that you need physical confidence to play soccer, and one good way of building this is to practise a bodily contact game with your pals.

I used to play a game of 'steal ball' with one of my friends – who went to West Brom with me when we were both boys – and it helped us tremendously. The idea of the game is simple. I have to get the ball off him in a confined area, while he has to shield it, turn and hold off my challenge. It must be played in a small area because the idea isn't to run away with the ball but to hold off the tackle.

The trick is to get the ball on the outside of the foot that's further away from the challenger, and put the whole of your body between the ball and the tackler. By holding your arm slightly bent, and making sure that your non-playing leg is firmly on the ground, you can hold him off while he tries to toe-poke the ball out of your control. The side of your body that's in contact with the opponent must be tensed, so that arm, shoulder, and leg are

forming a wall against his challenge.

A fair soccer challenge must be shoulder to shoulder, and in 'steal ball' you both have the opportunity to develop this. If your opponent is much bigger and stronger he's going to push you out of the way, so you have to improve your own strength and work out ways of withstanding such physical pressures.

This can be done only with hard work. You must train regularly, exercise daily, and practise whenever you can. And as well as developing skill you must build up your confidence to take the knocks in the game. It all adds to your success and enjoyment in the end.

An opponent strikes from the side. I use my shoulder to hold him off, strengthening my defence by bending my elbow and holding my arm rigid.

WEIGHTS AND ROUTINES

❝ Equipment for weight training isn't all that important. If you haven't got access to any, say at the local sports hall or gymnasium, improvise if you want to use weights. You can get the same effect by tying small bags filled with sand around your ankles as you do your normal leg exercises for increasing strength **❞**

Weight-training is an area of exercise which is not too important for younger players, whose general fitness should be reasonably high, but once boys get over 15 or so then the use of weights can be of advantage.

When I was a young player at West Bromwich the coaching staff were worried about my size and put me onto a programme which not only included the use of weights, but also involved drinking a bottle of beer every day!

This may sound strange, but there are properties in a bottle of stout which will help develop the body, and this combined with exercise seemed to do the trick.

The very mention of weight-training usually brings two reactions. People think either that weight-training means weight-lifting and conjure up visions of massive weight-lifters grunting and groaning as they haul huge loads above their heads, or that such equipment will be another load on their wallet.

As far as soccer is concerned neither applies. Weight-training means completing a routine of exercises using equipment which has to be lifted, pushed, or pulled by the body, arms or legs, but it does not mean that you have to use any very heavy weights or be competitive.

Most sports and leisure centres have weight-training facilities and experts on hand to advise, but be careful and remember you want to use the weights for fitness and building strength, not turn yourself into a shape that is totally unsuited for soccer.

Do-it-yourself weight-training

As far as expense is concerned, if you want to use weights as part of a training routine then there's no need for them to cost you anything at all, apart from a few pence.

Two small bags, tied together and filled with a little sand, can have the same effect on leg raising exercises as hydraulic bench-weights would. Just drape the bags over your feet, lie on the floor and raise your legs; provided that the bags aren't too heavy they'll do the trick.

Any small solid object which can be held in the hand – a paperweight, piece of metal, or a large spanner – can be used in arm-raising exercises, and it's very easy to improvise with everyday objects if you find that the routine work-out isn't having its required effect.

However, before turning to the use of weights I think that it's important for any player to be able to get through a simple set of exercises to give him

some ides of the standard of fitness he's reached, or is trying to achieve.

Strength and stamina

Here's a short routine aimed at the average amateur footballer of any age group. It's the sort of exercise work-out you should go through each day, but its length may be extended, or in some cases shortened, if it's not right.

Let me stress once again that the aim is for fitness, strength and stamina. If you cannot complete the routine, rest and then continue. Next time see how far you get without the rest and you'll see how you've improved. If you find the routine easy, then increase the number of repetitions.

● Begin by lying on the floor, legs together, with your arms stretched back above your head. Sit up and lean forward, touching your toes, then lie back again. Repeat this ten times.

● Roll over onto your front and complete five press-ups.

● Return to your starting position, but with both knees bent and feet flat on the floor. Place both hands flat on your thighs and rise from the floor with shoulders and head, touching your knees with your forehead. Repeat this ten times.

● Turn over again and complete five press-ups.

● From the press-ups return to the starting position and complete another ten sit-ups, but this time instead of leaning forward from the sitting position twist to the left five times, then the right five times, with your hands linked behind your head.

● Another five press-ups completes the short routine.

N.B. This set of exercises will exercise most of your upper body, especially the stomach area, and will give you a fair idea of your fitness.

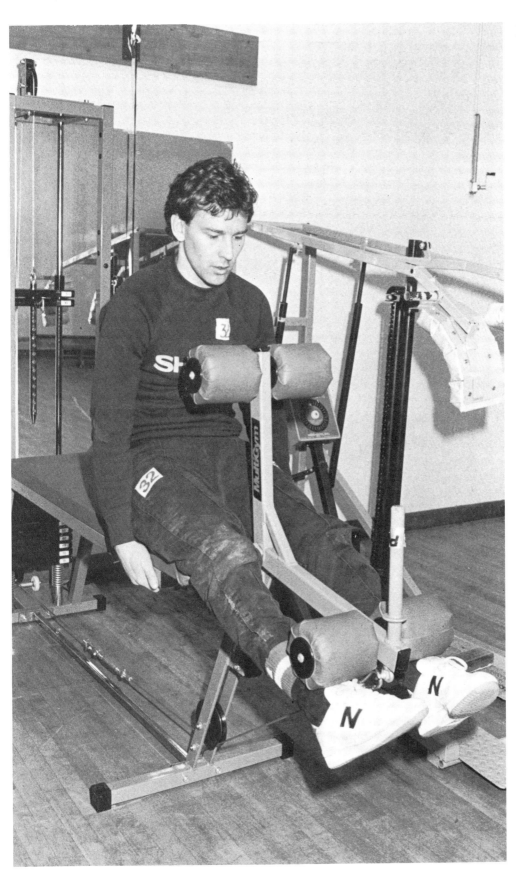

Gymnasium weight-training equipment can be used to strengthen all parts of the body. This simple bench has weights attached which develop leg muscles.

TRAINING ALONE

❝ When training on your own remember that you're your own judge. If you're trying to strengthen a particular area of your game, or build up a specific part of your body, then you must work at it – and not take the easy way out by convincing yourself that you've done enough, when you know that you haven't! ❞

One of the hardest parts of keeping fit is training alone. It's so easy to put it off till tomorrow, and that's where determination comes in. If you want to succeed at the game you mustn't give up. So, if you can turn a solo session into something you can enjoy, you won't mind being on your own.

The simplest practice session for any would-be soccer player is to get out with a ball at your feet and just develop your control skills. A chalked target on a wall can provide you with something to aim at with either a shot or a pass or a chip, and running with the ball in close control will aid your dribbling ability.

Keeping the ball in the air with your head and feet, and rebounding it off the wall, will also strengthen control and heading ability, and if there is a convenient wall to run and 'pass' the ball against you can practise picking up at speed. You can also see where the term 'wall pass' came from!

Using your imagination

It's easy to brighten up a solo session by conjuring up an imaginary opponent. Ten consecutive headers against the wall is a goal for your side, fewer than ten a goal for the opposition, and a little bit of fun like that quickly adds to all-round skill.

Some sports are easy to practise when you're on your own, like golf for example. A golfer takes a bag of balls along to a practice area and hits them, but with soccer it's not quite that easy.

But there are areas of your game where you can work on your own, and ball exercises added to the work-out can break up the monotony of a training routine.

One of the simplest forms of developing ball control is to set yourself an obstacle course which you have to run through while keeping the ball at your feet. It doesn't need to be too sophisticated: half a dozen empty plant pots (the plastic ones!) spread down the garden at three- or four-foot intervals can provide the perfect 'opposition' for a solo game.

Starting with your back to the pots and the ball in front of you the object is to turn, and run through the obstacles passing one on the left, the next on the right and so on until you are at the far

Right: Practise ball skills whenever you have the time. Here I'm heading the ball against a wall in a simple solo training routine.

Far right: Keeping the ball in the air, playing it from foot to foot is a way of developing control.

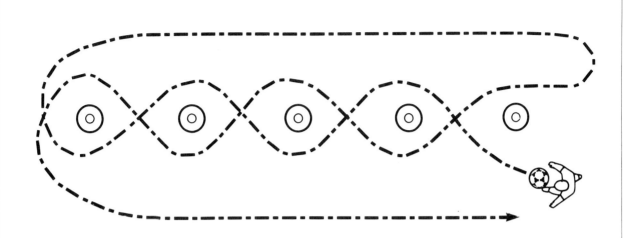

You can make a slalom course out of any solid objects. Aim to run in and out of the row without losing control of the ball and without touching the obstacles. At the end turn and sprint back down the outside still controlling the ball. Vary the exercise by running back through the course and sprinting back down the opposite side.

end, then sprint back along the outside keeping the ball under control all the time.

If you touch an obstacle it's a goal for the opposition, but if not then your side has scored. The object of the exercise is controlling the ball at speed, so if you have a watch it's a good idea to time a run and then see if you can beat it.

Playing air-ball

Keeping the ball in the air is another good solo exercise. You start by getting the ball onto the upper part of one foot, pulling it back with the sole of the foot, then flicking it up with your toes until it is airborne. Then it's a case of getting alternate feet under the ball as it drops. This develops a vital 'feel' for the ball as well as strengthening your non-kicking foot.

Many young players have seen top names juggling with a ball in this way and probably don't realize that they have already reached a high standard in other aspects of the game. It's obviously great fun to be able to flick the ball from foot to foot, thigh to thigh and roll it across the back of your neck and down your shoulders and arms, and this is something which requires great skill – but it isn't much good if you can't hit an accurate pass ten yards!

Air-ball is a good game to play on your own; every time the ball hits the ground you lose a goal, and for every ten times you touch it off the ground you score!

ROBSON'S TIPS

● *A great way of taking the boredom out of solo training is to keep each part of the programme short, and to vary each exercise either with or without a ball.*

● *Remember that the only way you're going to make the grade as a soccer player is by hard work. You must develop skill and fitness, because one is no good without the other.*

● *Most youngsters have vivid imaginations and it isn't too difficult for them to conjure up games to play with a soccer ball if they're on their own, and it's surprising how you can develop skill without a partner. But it's also easy to give in if there's no-one around to encourage you, so you must have strong willpower.*

Training alone means that it's difficult for you to practise every area of the game. It isn't possible to hit a long ball or challenge an opponent, for example. But with a bit of imagination you can enjoy yourself as you improve.

GROUP TRAINING

A group of youngsters can put their skills to practise in a competitive atmosphere just by dividing into two teams with makeshift goals. That's really what practice should be all about when you're a kid. When you join a club you'll start organized training sessions – but junior soccer should really be fun

Group training can obviously be more enjoyable than working out on your own. When there are a few of you then ball games become more fun, and even exercises don't seem to present the obstacle they might when you have only yourself for company.

Nowadays there are probably more qualified coaches than there have been at any other time in the game's history, so it's possible that even a small junior club will have a coach who knows enough about the game to pass on some good advice to young players.

I've said this earlier in the book and I think it's worth a second mention: the aim of every junior club coach must be to see that the players in his control get enjoyment out of soccer. It's not for him to ram tactics and technicalities down the throats of his players, but to get them playing soccer and coming back for more.

That can make the difference between a successful side and one which struggles. If the players aren't happy in their training and practice sessions then they'll show it on the field. The more they want to play, the more they will respond.

Making practice fun

Even at top level it's surprising how players will respond to new ideas which take some of the routine out of training sessions. Remember that the average professional trains two hours every day, and if you've been in the game for over ten years that's a lot of hard work. It can easily become a case of going through the motions if you're not careful.

The same thing can apply at junior level. If youngsters have been to school all day and have been working hard in the classroom, the last thing they want to do is go along to their soccer training and find themselves faced with a blackboard and a lot of complicated diagrams.

So the emphasis on group training should be to get the most out of the players and to put the fun back into their game.

One of the simplest methods of group training is to go down to the local park with a bunch of pals and simply have a game of soccer. You don't need all the equipment; coats or trees will form goals and any number of players on each side will give you the chance to develop your skills and try them out in competitive conditions.

This is a natural progression from working on your skills alone. The tricks and techniques you've developed in practice can be tried out and

ROBSON'S TIPS

● *Group training should involve ball games as much as possible even if they are played with the hands rather than the feet. These help to keep players alert. Long running and exercise routines can become boring.*

● *Nobody can teach an individual how to get the best out of group training sessions; he knows whether or not he's pushing himself or taking it easy. If you don't give 100 per cent you'll suffer in the end – don't blame the coach.*

● *Coaches should vary group training routines as much as they can. Even if they're not qualified they can have some idea of the standard of fitness they're trying to attain in their players, and those in charge of junior teams must concentrate on getting youngsters to enjoy playing.*

new ideas picked up from friends. But essentially you should have a good time.

When a young player joins a soccer club he will find that organized training is usually just as much fun as the kick around in the park. Most amateur clubs have a couple of nights a week when they meet to go through exercises and play some kind of game, whether it is five-a-side or head tennis.

The person in charge may not be a qualified coach but he should have the knowledge of the sort of routine which help players achieve fitness and have a selection of ball-games which develop their skills.

Tunnel ball

Gymnasium games like tunnel-ball are variations on training patterns which can develop areas of the game even if you don't use your feet. Tunnel ball is a simple game, and one you've probably played at school.

I think every soccer club plays it during training at some time during the season.

A row of players stand with legs open in two teams of equal numbers. The front player in each team has a ball and he leans forward and rolls it through the legs to the back player, who picks it up and sprints to the front. The action is repeated

Equipment doesn't need to be sophisticated. A game of head tennis can be played without using a net. Here a piece of cord is stretched across the gymnasium. The same game could be played out of doors using a similar 'net'.

until each player in the row has been to the front and the team which completes the sequence first are the winners.

I always feel that this sort of game is much better for players than simply going on training runs. It's very easy to shut off your mind on a run and just plod on, and as top players are quite fit anyway the running is no hardship, but activity games get the mind working as well and competition means a lively session.

So coaches must always be on the lookout for ball games which can brighten up the mundane, make their players concentrate, and look forward to the next session.

TRAINING ROUTINES

❝ I don't care whether it's at top professional level or with a local junior club – it's very important that coaches vary training. If the players at the junior club know that every week they're going to play head-tennis, do some press-ups then go on a two-mile run, they'll get bored pretty quickly. So if coaches don't have any new ideas it's up to the players to suggest some and make life more interesting **❞**

I'm often asked just what professional players do with their time during a week. The question has usually come from someone who knows very little about soccer and who obviously has the impression that all we do is roll up on a Saturday and play the game. Nothing could be further from reality, and anyone who thinks that soccer is an easy life can think again.

Most top clubs train along similar lines: two hours each morning, sometimes a specialist session in the afternoon (set-piece play, goal-keeper work-outs) and one day off between Monday and Saturday plus Sunday if you're not injured or called in for extra training. Even holidays like Christmas Day, New Year and Good Friday mean training, with games the next day, and when there's a holiday Monday during the season we will be in on the Sunday!

With all that training it's obvious that the routines we use have to be as varied as possible and designed not only to get or keep you fit but also to occupy your mind and entertain you. There's nothing worse than boring sessions in which even the most dedicated professionals find themselves thinking about something other than the task in hand, and the good coaches make sure this doesn't happen.

Any serious training session should always begin with a 20-minute warm-up comprising the type of exercises we have dealt with in the last sections: press-ups, squat-thrusts, leg raising, stretching and stomach exercises all aimed at getting your body ready for a rigorous work-out. This would of course be shorter for younger players.

The coach should then divide the players into two groups of equal numbers and the next half-an-hour or so is taken up with some kind of football game.

One-touch football

One of the favourites of top level clubs is one-touch, and it's as straightforward as it sounds. Each player is allowed just one touch of the ball as it comes to him, and with no controlling touch and no dribbling it's a fast furious game – and it means a lot of running 'off the ball' to get into good positions to pick up instant passes from your colleagues. It also develops the first touch so essential in good players. If you have to jab around at the ball to get it under control an opponent is going to take it off you.

One-touch can be increased to two or three

One-touch football develops quick thinking and fast reaction. Play it in a confined area for maximum effect.

depending on the skill of the players, but not many more than that because it becomes difficult for the coach – who is refereeing – to decide if a player is going too far and having a touch too many!

Another interesting game is to have *three* teams playing on the pitch at the same time with perhaps the odd player dropping out for a few minutes. If there are 16 players in the group they split into three groups of five, and the spare man stands down.

The groups – say, reds, whites and blues – start with reds defending one goal and blues the other and whites can attack at either end. This means that at any time reds and blues can come under attack from not just the whites but the side defending at the other end who push players forward. However when the attack loses the ball and the defence breaks clear, the whites change sides and attack at the other end.

This always puts strikers on the attack and gives defenders the opportunity to defend if the teams are selected in the right way.

Staying bright

It's ideas like this that keep players' minds bright. When a player is being asked to report for training day after day it can become a chore, but if he can be made to look forward to it, it makes all the difference.

Coaches of amateur and junior clubs should take note of this because really their job is harder. In professional soccer the players have already gone through the early stages of the game; we've all played for junior and school sides, and some of us for amateur clubs before we became apprentices and then professionals. We know what it takes to get to the stage where we can earn a good living by playing the game and we know that if we skip training or slacken off then

we'll be out of work. If an amateur loses interest he can find another way of filling his time even though he may regret it later in life, so coaches have to keep on their toes.

Small clubs may not have many more than a dozen players, and if this is the case then a game of five-a-side can help, and if they wanted to develop the three-team game they could use any spare men in the centre of the field as the changing attackers.

If you have only one goal to kick at – it may be that you share a park pitch or train against a gym wall – then there are many other games you can try. Three corners are a penalty; change round at five; score and swap round, change keepers every goal with each player taking a turn – the variations are endless.

Use a ball

We have a unique game with the England team where we have *four* goals to attack and defend! Using five-a-side goals set up on the flanks we divide into two teams and can score either at each end or in the goals on the touchline. This means that you have to defend the flanks as well as the normal end of the field and it gives players plenty to think about as well as lots of involvement.

Before this game starts you decide which end you're attacking and which flank, and defend the two opposite goals. It sounds like chaos, but it's great fun.

I think I should also stress my feeling that group training should always be done with a ball if possible. Exercises are good for warming up, or perhaps to tone down after a good work-out, but players will do much more running without realizing it if there's a ball involved.

The goals have been shortened to make scoring more difficult and even the keeper is allowed just one attempt to save. If he fails to collect cleanly he has to wait for another player to touch the ball.

BUILDING STAMINA

❝ When players are young they enjoy having a game of soccer and that is why they find it very hard when they get to a professional club and discover that a lot of time is spent on building their strength and their stamina. Getting out of bed in the morning, working out all day and then being so tired that they have to go to bed early seems a long way from the glamour they expected. So you need stamina in your mind as well as your body to get through periods like that, which are so important in later life ❞

It was only when I reached professional level that I realized what an important part stamina played in the game. When I was an amateur – before joining West Brom as an apprentice – I played with a local side and loved every minute of it . . . but I paid little attention to stamina or endurance.

With the amateur side I looked forward to one or two training sessions a week when we would play five-a-side, and then the weekend game. During the match if I got a bit tired then I'd take a rest, changing from a run into a gentle trot, and even standing still to get my wind back. What a shock I got when I became a full-time player!

During top-level games there's no standing still, apart from the odd second or two. You have to run for the whole 90 minutes, and longer when games include extra time.

Professional players get the stamina to do this simply through training. Because they work hard every day their bodies will take the strain of running more or less flat out for an hour of every 90-minute game, with the other half hour taken up by slower pace running.

Tough going
Many players – some who've even reached the top level – have given up the game because they didn't have the stamina to last the pace of a 90-minute professional game. They might have had terrific skill, but they hated training and couldn't stand the thought of having to run every day to build up stamina, so they packed in.

I actually *like* doing it, but I know what hard work it is and every young player has to realize how tough the road ahead is if he wants to make it.

Some players will even go running on a Sunday when there's no training session, to relax! I find that swimming gives me the relaxation I need after a game and that's what I like to do on a Sunday. It's a different type of exercise, and it gets rid of any aches and pains from the day before.

Routine stamina building for a young player should be a programme of exercises and running each day. It may mean that he has to work-out after school in the early evening so he has to make sure that he has the time to do homework and other tasks his parents may have for him.

I'd say that he has to build up his routine to achieve a work-out time of around an hour and a half each evening. This can be divided into exercise and running and designed so that the programme isn't the same every day.

ROBSON'S TIPS

● *Players should aim for around 90 minutes exercise and running a day, but build up to it – don't start at that length straight away.*

● *Eating the right food is essential. Mix your diet and try to eat meals that contain less fat: try a jacket potato instead of a plate of chips, for example.*

● *Work out your own training routine and vary it each day so that it doesn't become a bore. This is how you'll build stamina to give you staying power during a game.*

Soccer crazy
I played soccer virtually every night when I was a boy. I would come home from school, do my homework and then go out and play soccer with my pals for a couple of hours, and even though I didn't realize it I was building up stamina through regular exercise.

What I've discovered is that the more running you do when you are younger then the more good it does you when you get older.

Boys who are good at cross-country and long distance running when they are younger will usually have the stamina for soccer as they get into their late teens. You must have regular exercise and the determination to succeed, even though it is hard work.

When I first went to West Brom I honestly felt like packing it all in after a couple of years. They put me on programmes which included weight training, running and exercise every day and kept insisting that I was too small. Then it would be more weights and more running and it started to get to me. I was hardly playing any soccer, just working on my body all the time, but when I look back now I can see the importance of it all. It did me a lot of good and gave me strength and stamina for the professional game.

Eating for fitness
Another routine that you must get into is eating the right sort of food. In general young boys can eat almost anything that they fancy, because they shouldn't have any sort of weight problems if they get enough exercise during a day, since any

excess they put on they will burn off as they run around. But it is important that you try to eat the right sort of food to give you energy without putting on fat.

Variety is the important thing here, and the more varied your diet the better. I know that chips are usually at the top of every youngster's list when it comes to favourite foods, but if you replace them with the odd salad, or have a jacket potato you'll feel the benefit.

There are many books on health diets and that sort of thing, and I'm not proposing that everyone who reads this should want to change their eating habits all that much. But it's important to get the right sort of food. You need protein and you can get this in many ways and there are vital vitamins in fresh fruit, vegetables, eggs and cheese.

Any would-be soccer player will know if he's overweight and he'll soon know if he hasn't got the stamina to keep up with his pals!

A programme for stamina building should consist of weight training, exercise and running, coupled with the right sort of food. If you want to live on beefburgers and sweets you might have problems!

Manchester United players warm up before pre-match training. Sessions the day before a game are usually kept to light exercise and simple ball work, but professional players train for many hours each week to reach and maintain peak fitness.

SPEED TRAINING

❝ So many young players think they're quick over a few yards, but they're not really – they're just average. You have to train hard to get the edge over your opponent, because getting there first – whether in defence or attack – is so often the difference between success and failure in soccer ❞

In this section of the book I would like to introduce you to my 'doggie'. No, I'm not going to talk about my pet mongrel, or get you to take the dog for a walk, but tell you about the 'doggie' who will help you to develop the running speed so essential to your game.

'Doggie' is the name given to an exercise developed many years ago in soccer and now used at just about every soccer club. Sometimes players shudder at the prospect of a session of 'doggies', but there's nothing to be afraid of – unless you're scared of getting fit.

Now when you think about it a player runs almost continuously during a game, but not at one pace. He runs in short bursts usually of no more than 30 yards and quite often no longer than four or five yards. It's explosive stuff – high speed from a standing start.

At situations like a free kick and a throw-in a player might run in one direction, then turn and burst the other way to throw off an opponent or chase the player with the ball, so we have to have an exercise which will provide players with this sort of movement. And exercising with doggies gives us just that.

Strength for speed

Strength is important in speed work, because you'll need that speed many times during a game. You have to make sure that you develop good body strength and build up your legs through regular exercise and weight training. You're looking for all round fitness, and you'll certainly have it tested to the full with 'doggies'.

Imagine you're standing on the goal-line on a pitch which is 110 yards long. For this exercise we're going to use just half the pitch and the lines of the six-yard box are the markers we aim for first. At a signal you sprint from the goal-line to the edge of the goal area, and then turn and sprint back to the starting line. Not bad was it – just a sharp sprint of 12 yards.

Next we run to the edge of the penalty area and back, a round trip of 36 yards, and finally to the halfway line and back – and that's 110 yards. If we put a marker half way between the halfway line and the penalty area we can add to the variations. A full run is goal-line, six-yard line and back; goal-line, penalty area and back; goal-line, 35-yard marker and back; and finally goal-line, halfway line and back.

If you think it sounds easy, try it. Then do it again, and this time run to the far goal-line and back as well, and always at a sprint. Now the idea

ROBSON'S TIPS

● 'Doggies' give you sprinting and stamina work all in one. The short shuttles are explosive, while the longer legs are for staying power.

● Work on rapid leg pumping action as part of sprint training; see how many times you can pump your feet up and down in a minute as you run on the spot. You're looking for explosive sprinting power.

● Take a rest between exercises when sprint training. The idea is for you to run flat out each time, not simply to complete the routine. You'll quickly build up strength and may not need as many rest breaks in the next session.

● The thigh and hamstring muscles are the most important for sprinting, so do exercises which strengthen them and use weights to build power.

● If you know you're a bit sluggish on the pitch, work extra hard at speed training: it'll make a big difference to your game.

is not to run till you drop, but to run flat out every time, even if you rest in between.

Short steps

For high-speed running you must develop your thigh and hamstring muscles – the muscles on the front and back of the upper half of your leg. Running by using very short steps is one way of giving them extra work to do, and it's a good exercise to try in training.

It also helps you to learn to pump your feet quickly to get moving fast from a standing start and shows you how a shortened stride comes into a sprint rather than a loping leg movement.

I've seen players training with two rows of car tyres placed on the ground and running so that they step inside each tyre – one row for each leg – in another illustration of the shorter leg action. Running up and downstairs is another – but be careful. So when training for speed look for the explosive start, the quick turn and the short step – and remember that 'doggies' are good for you!

Left: Doggies – I'm competing with a colleague shuttle running using cones placed 5, 10, 15 and 25 yards apart.

Below left: Rapid on-the-spot running develops leg strength and should be carried out in short bursts with a rest between.

Below right: Many people have cycling machines nowadays and they're a great way of building up leg strength and helping all-round fitness.

RUNNING FOR SOCCER

‘ Of all the exercises we use in training I think 'running for soccer' is the one which makes you feel as if you've taken part in a game. It incorporates every movement you use in the course of a career in soccer, and all in one circuit of a pitch. At least it seems that way, and if the coach uses his imagination he can make it interesting as well as stamina testing for his players ₅

What's the difference between a top athlete and a professional soccer player? Both train every day, both are used to pushing their bodies to the limit and, physical contact apart, the athlete and the soccer player are similar in many ways. But the type of running used in soccer is nothing like that in athletics.

I've already looked at explosive sprinting and the way that 'doggies' can help, and now we come to my favourite exercise session – running for soccer.

This isn't really the best name for a session like this, but it gives you the kind of stamina-sapping work-out you'll get during a normal game. And it can be very enjoyable if the coach has a good imagination.

I wouldn't like to guess how far a player actually runs during a game but I would reckon that it would be several miles, with some of it at high speed. That's why you cannot really make a comparison with a runner taking part in an athletics event.

Running four or five miles means sticking to a steady pace lap after lap; taking part in the 400 metres requires a strong sprint for one circuit of a track; sprinting 100 metres is a flat out burst along a straight line. But in a game of soccer you will do none of those things.

Your running is all done in bursts, and in between those bursts there is jumping, throwing, sliding, leaping, charging, twisting, kicking and many other actions, so running for soccer has to contain every aspect of the game.

A match without a ball

It starts with the coach in the centre of a ring of players, and after a warm-up session they jog slowly for a few minutes loosening arms, shoulders and legs by running on the spot and shaking each limb.

Then we begin a series of bending exercises, a jog, a trot and then more on-the-spot work. The coach demands a sprint, then calls a halt. Players have to pull up as quickly as possible without risking any strains and he can then order a sprint in the opposite direction, followed by a slow walk. Then, on the coach's command, it's off on a short-step run, another halt and then ten knee-jumps – perhaps backwards this time, leaping in the air and bringing the knees up to the chest. Then it's another sprint, ten press-ups, a walk, then a jog. And so on. The variations are endless and the session can go on for as long as the coach thinks fit – and fit's the right word. If you aren't

you soon will be!

This is a soccer match without a ball and it's surprising how much energy and concentration it requires. If you sprint 30 yards then leap up to head an imaginary football 10 times, jog 50 yards then do 10 squat-thrusts followed by another sprint, not only does it build strength and stamina, but it also keeps you alert, because you're waiting to respond to the next command.

Competitive running

Another part of running for soccer is to have the players form two lines of equal or near-equal numbers and to race one another slalom style, taking it in turns to compete. The first runners set off on the word go and weave in and out of their team until they reach the end. Then they sprint back to the starting position and release the next runner.

This type of race increases competitiveness and also reproduces another example of running during a game when a player will be trying to dodge his way past opponents.

Of course fitness for soccer can also come in handy for other sports, and there's no doubt that after a session of running for soccer players will know just what level of fitness they've reached. Coaches should try to stick to just one circuit of a full-size pitch when taking players on a session like this, but of course they can cover a great deal of ground, by sending them back on reverse direction runs . . . and I can tell you there's nothing worse than thinking you've reached the end and hearing the words, 'Right then, now turn and sprint in the opposite direction!'

It may seem like torture at the time, but it pays dividends in the long run, if you know what I mean!

ROBSON'S TIPS

● *It's always advisable to get players warmed up before doing anything too strenuous. Jogging, running on-the-spot and short sprints are ideal before press-ups, knee-jumps or squat-thrusts.*

● *'Running for soccer' can build up stamina in every area provided that the coach makes his session varied enough to incorporate plenty of exercises.*

Top left: Running for soccer – a session of knee jumps during group training.

Centre left: Still in the same circuit, the players complete a series of press-ups.

Bottom left: On the command 'sprint' the players set off on a short run before going into another part of the routine.

SKILL TESTS

❝ Competition is the basis of soccer, and training games which have a competitive edge are ideal for testing the skills of players. Finding out how good – or bad – you are at certain ball skills can be of great value to a player. If you can't do a particular test, then you have to work harder to achieve the standard set by your team-mates. But if you're good at such tests then you must work hard to improve your ability still more. No matter how good you are there's never time to sit back and admire yourself! ❞

Giving players skill tests by introducing a competitive element into training sessions is another way that coaches can help to develop the talents of their squad as well as offering another alternative to basic exercise routines and ball-work.

Even the most junior teams can benefit from skill-testing sessions because not only do they show the coach which of his players have the most ability, but they also inspire those who may lag behind to practise and get themselves up to a reasonable standard.

It's only when players meet at school or youth club level that they really get to know their own potential or the standard of skill they have achieved. It's only by comparing themselves with others that players will know if they're playing at the right level, or if they should work harder to reach the same standard as their friends.

Many of the summer soccer schools have incorporated a scoring system into skill tests so that they can select the player who is top of the class. I don't think that there's anything wrong with this – provided that the youngsters who finish lower down are coached and encouraged to help them improve.

Testing times

The tests described in this section are really aimed at players who want to discover their own standard, and to give coaches some idea of the methods they can use to encourage players to develop their ball skills.

The simplest test, using the least sophisticated piece of equipment, is one which many youngsters will probably have tried without realizing its importance.

Using an object similar to a child's paddling pool – a circle of coats, a large carboard box, etc – the idea is to chip the ball into the container or circle from various distances. You should start from about 15 feet and increase the length after several kicks. Working in a group this can be great fun, especially if you have enough players to divide into two teams with a point scored every time you hit the target.

A skill test used at professional level is to reduce the size of the goal by placing a cone, or sticking a corner flag, about six feet from one of the posts. You can only score – without a goalkeeper – if you get the ball between the marker and the upright. Again working on increasing distances, shooting can be from anywhere within one half of the field.

Shooting practice

In my days at West Brom the coach introduced me to a great skill-testing game which we played a lot in pre-season practice.

From one corner of the penalty area we had to shoot at the area of net between the far post and the stanchion; if the ball hit the back of the net it didn't count. We had to use the right foot from the right-hand edge of the box and shoot into the left-hand netting, and then reverse the process from the left. The ball has to hit the netting without touching the ground and it's a good test of accurate shooting.

Another simple but effective test is to get players to chip the ball from the edge of the penalty area, or again from increasing distances, and bounce if off the crossbar.

The secret of success

I know that the idea of the 'real' game is to miss the bar, but it's surprising how much fun you can have aiming for it in practice. And I can let you into a secret: this is one of the games many top players play towards the end of a training session. Even a lot of my England pals will get in a group and try to outpoint each other with 10 or 20 chips apiece.

Any coach worth his salt should try to get his players involved in this sort of game. It may seem a bit simple, but it gets team spirit going and players love to compete against each other.

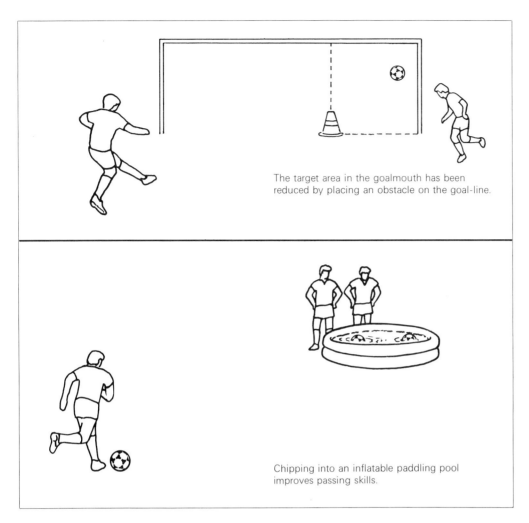

The target area in the goalmouth has been reduced by placing an obstacle on the goal-line.

Chipping into an inflatable paddling pool improves passing skills.

Of course the reason behind any skill test is to improve and demonstrate the player's ability, but it also helps to develop different areas of play and is an extension to a training session.

Playing in pairs

Training in pairs gives players another opportunity to test their skill with simple games. Starting ten yards apart, player A flicks the ball in the air once, and passes to player B, who flicks the ball up once and returns it. Player A now flicks it up twice and passes it again. Then it's three flicks, four and so on, a good level to reach being around ten touches without the ball bouncing on the ground before the pass is made.

You can use the same game to strengthen and test heading ability, nodding from one to another when working in pairs; or you can play the narrow goal game again, this time getting the ball between the post and the marker with your head. This needs a player to send over accurate crosses as the rest of the squad heads at the smaller target.

Developing accuracy

The idea of using the smaller section of the goal is to develop accuracy. It's quite easy to hit an empty goal, but when the target area is reduced it makes players concentrate more on the part of the game they're working on.

Any skill test like this can have its uses in the game itself and you can see the value of heading or shooting at a smaller section of the goal because during a match that is perhaps the size of target you'll actually have, given that defenders and the keeper may be 'in the way'.

'Skittleball'

Another simple target game – and a development of the paddling pool idea I mentioned earlier – is to have several circles or squares of cones placed around the penalty area. These can be reduced in size until there's just one skittle in the centre, and players score ten if they knock over the middle marker, five if they hit the circle it stands in and so on, down to one for dropping the ball in the outer rim of cones. This skill is ideal for testing the lofted pass. Chip the ball from a fixed distance to land first bounce in the target to score.

If you try out these games they'll give you some idea of the standard of skill you've reached, and I'm sure that you will come up with some other tests yourself as you develop your ability.

SPEED TESTS

> ❛ I'm all for making training sessions fun. Running about all the time might get you fit, but if there's a competitive edge to it, if you are running against somebody, then it will develop your own will to win and make it more enjoyable ❜

A short sprint from a sitting start. Players have been told to sit with hands on knees until the word 'go'.

After testing his skill a player should next look at his ability to run at speed and his stamina to last the full length of a game. Just as we did with skill, it's possible for players to try out various speed tests which will prove the standard reached, and give an idea of the improvement needed to stay ahead of or catch up with others in the team or squad.

These tests also provide coaches with a way of varying running sessions during training.

Shuttle-running, as used in the 'doggies' described on page 108, is one way of getting players to race against one another in a form of football running. But one type of race to be avoided is the straightforward 100 metres sprint from starting blocks to finishing line – because as far as soccer is concerned this is totally foreign to the running you do during the game.

Variations on a theme
The simplest sprint for soccer is over about 20 yards, but coaches can add a number of conditions to the dash to make it interesting and extra competitive.

Instead of a standing start, try sitting it out! Yes, you start with the competitors sitting on the ground and on the word go they have to get up and sprint to the finishing marker. This might sound a little weird, but it happens time and time again during a game that a player will find himself on the ground, having to get up and run after an opponent or into a better position. But you won't find him on any starting blocks!

Another variation is the lying start, with runners actually lying flat on their backs, or in the press-up position, waiting for the starting signal.

A lot of running tests are used by soccer clubs during the build-up to the start of a season, when coaches are trying to make sure that players are back to peak fitness. Once the season is under way coaching tends to be about certain aspects of the game itself and the development of set-piece play, but there's no doubt about the value of competitive running.

Hands up!
Another sprint start we use at Manchester United is for players to sit on the ground with their legs

crossed and hands on their head. They have to start their sprint from this position without touching the ground with their hands as they get up!

It might sound a long way from playing soccer but it isn't. Such tests develop agility as well as speed and they also help players to build up a good sense of balance. If you're falling slightly as you try to set off in a sprint you need to be able to recover quickly and get running correctly just as you would if knocked off balance by an opponent.

Jump-starting

We also use a star-jump start. For this the two opposing runners face each other and jump legs astride, arms raised until the coach says go. He can let them do a number of jumps or might decide to start them after just one, so this type of test keeps the players on their toes in more ways than one!

This sort of thing brings fun into training instead of players simply doing a series of short sprints.

We even have a running game where players can tug and pull at each other to try to prevent the other one from winning. It's intended to help to develop awareness of bodily contact.

During an actual game an opponent will try to block a run by getting in your way, putting his arm across you, and even holding onto your shirt. We do this to each other in a sprint game but that's as far as it should go; you mustn't trip each other up or tackle one another – just try

to prevent the opponent from getting off to a good start.

When it comes to real bodily contact one game we play is for pairs of roughly the same build to jump into each other, shoulder to shoulder, making contact in the air but without a ball. This develops the physical contact side of the sport and is very valuable to young players.

Getting up from a sitting position and breaking into a sprint happens often during a game. Sprint exercises such as this test strength and agility.

KIT SELECTION AND CARE

❜ During the 1986 World Cup I saw some players who wore 'shin-pads' on the backs of their legs to protect their calf muscles. I don't think this is necessary, but I'd always recommended that any player wears shin-pads for normal protection. A kick on the shin is the easiest injury to pick up, and the easiest to avoid, so protect yourself **❟**

Right: The modern player wears lightweight top-quality equipment. Here I am in the Manchester United dressing-room with the kit I wear on match days.

Far right: Shin-guards are essential. This type protects the ankle as well as the front of the leg but is still light enough not to impede.

What's the most important part of a soccer player's kit? Ask any leading professional and he'll tell you straight away that he pays extra attention when selecting his boots.

That rule should also apply to any young player hoping to do well at any level of the game. If you don't have a good pair of boots which fit you correctly then you won't be able to get the most out of your game.

There's never been a better selection of equipment and that includes boots, and I would say that provided you stick to the well-known makes you won't go far wrong.

One of the problems young players face is that their feet are still growing when they get their first pair of boots. It isn't cheap for parents to buy new boots, and there's always the question of how quickly the youngsters will grow out of them.

From my own experience I would say that it's better for boots to be slightly too big than pinch a player's feet until he finds it hurts to wear them. He'll always grow into the boots and his game will improve as he gets older anyway, so if they're half an inch too big to start with this won't prove to be too much of a handicap for him.

Fit for play

Some manufacturers also cater for width as well as length fitting and I would recommend that parents go to a sports outfitters when buying boots, rather than just a high street shoeshop, where there may not be any really experienced staff around to give advice.

Once you have your boots there are two important things you must remember. First, new boots can hurt slightly to start with, even though nowadays they are made with much softer material than in the past.

At one time boots had to be soaked to soften them and make them fit. If I'd been writing this book 30 years ago or more I'd probably be advising you to put your boots on and put your feet in a bowl of water for an hour . . . but not today!

Now, when you wear new boots for the first time I'd advise you to rub a lubricant on your heels and toes to prevent them from blistering. It may feel a bit strange at first and I know that the first time I did it I thought it felt funny, but it's surprising how quickly you forget about it and get on with the game.

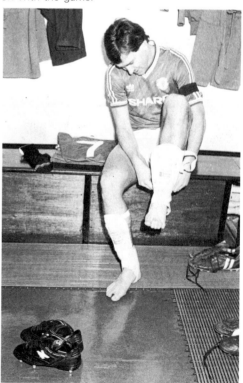

The second thing to remember is to tie them correctly. They mustn't be tied too tightly, or too loose. You want them to stay on and stay fastened, but not be so tight they hamper your circulation and cause cramp. It's also a good idea if you tuck the bows away underneath the lace around the boot so that the loops don't stick up. If they do it's very easy for an opponent's boot to catch your laces and even if all it does is untie them it can still be a problem. No, wrap the lace *round* and *under* the boot, then tie a bow on top and tuck the ends away out of sight.

Be prepared for plastic pitches

Studded boots are intended for use on grass and nowhere else. I know it's a great temptation for a youngster to put on his boots and trot out into the street with them but all he will do – as well as risking the danger of falling flat on his back – is ruin the studs. So never play on concrete in studded soccer boots; trainers are ideal for this type of surface.

Of course today we have plenty of synthetic pitches at schools, clubs and in parks and here a different type of boot is required. You can manage in ordinary trainers, but there is a boot with a sole designed specifically for synthetic or 'plastic' pitches. The boot has a pimpled sole with about 80 small 'studs', and these give you a reasonable grip while stopping you digging into the material and twisting your joints and ligaments when turning.

One thing I would strongly recommend for anyone playing on this type of artificial grass is to cover their arms and legs with a lubricant, especially the elbows and knees, to prevent friction burns from the material.

Self-protection

Protection is a vital part of the game and a player's protective equipment is usually confined to a pair of shin-pads. These are very important and I'd never let anyone play in a game I controlled without wearing them. They can prevent serious injury at any level, and no player should be without shin-guards. There are many different kinds on the market and even though they might feel uncomfortable to play in at first they're so valuable it's worth putting up with a little discomfort for the protection they offer.

Another way of protecting yourself from injury is to bandage your foot and ankle, or wear a specially designed 'sock' which helps strengthen your ankle. This prevents you twisting your ankle as you land after jumping or during a tackle, and it is very valuable especially as the modern boot is more like a shoe and offers no protection for your ankles.

Sock it to 'em!

At some junior clubs players have to provide their own kit, while others have only to use their own socks. I would say that if possible – apart from at top level – this is not a bad idea.

If you wear socks which haven't been washed properly they can rub your feet, but if you use your own each week then you'll know what sort of condition they're in and look after them. They should fit properly because if they don't they can cause rubbing and blisters, and they should always be tied up correctly at the top.

For this use a small piece of bandage wrapped around the sock just below the knee and tied at the side. It should be tied firmly but not too tightly, or it can restrict your circulation. Its job is to hold your sock up – nothing else – and it needs to be tied firmly enough to do that, and with the knot at the side and not on the front. This prevents it being pushed into the bone if you happen to get a kick there – which only adds to the pain!

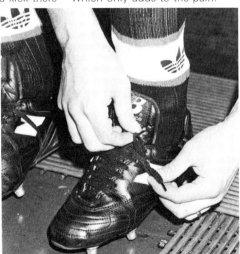

Boots should be tied firmly but not over-tight and the bows of the knot tucked into the lace to prevent them being snared by an opponent's studs.

MATCH-DAY PREPARATION

❝ Even the most experienced players have nerves on a match day. There's nothing unusual about having butterflies in your stomach before a game – in fact they can help to get your body in top gear – but they'll soon fly away once you start playing **❞**

Match day: the most important day in a player's week. Whether he's little Johnny Jones coming on as substitute for the scouts, or Bryan Robson leading England out at Wembley, match day is vitally important.

Everything has to be ready, and nothing can be left until tomorrow. Boots have to be cleaned and kit made ready for the match.

One rule I'd always lay down for amateur players is to give yourself plenty of time to prepare. There's nothing worse than rushing around at the last minute, and the biggest nuisance to any club is the player who arrives late, has to borrow gear off his pals, and is never ready when the referee calls the teams out. If he's unreliable as a timekeeper and can't remember to bring his own kit, how can you expect him to cope with the game itself?

Junior clubs and professional teams don't usually have this problem because they're well organized and have people who are responsible for making sure that players and kit are in the right place at the right time. But even then I know there are a lot of older players who will recognize a team-mate by the description I've just given!

It's no good for the player concerned, either. If you get in a state over your gear before the game, you're going to be in completely the wrong frame of mind to give anything like your best on the field.

Pre-match meals

Pre-match meals are important. Professionals don't usually eat anything within three hours of a match, but for youngsters this rule may not be of much importance. Most of them play on Saturday mornings, kicking off at about 10 o'clock and if they've had breakfast at 8.30 it won't do them any harm.

What you eat before a game is as important as when you eat it, and at Manchester United the rule is three hours before a game and nothing heavy. The usual menu is eggs, beans, cereals, and fish or chicken. No chips or burgers and only a light meal such as scrambled egg, beans on toast or perhaps a bowl of cornflakes. It has to be something light enough to be well digested before the game.

Another golden rule is to have plenty to drink before a game and once again this should be a

Right: Three hours before a game I tuck into a plate of scrambled eggs. Always avoid meals which will lie heavily on the stomach or be difficult to digest. Eggs, beans, toast, cornflakes or chicken are the choice of most players.

Far right: All dressed up and rarin' to go. Here I am in my Manchester United kit complete with captain's armband. Note how the dressing room has been prepared for match day with all kit ready for the players.

light drink such as orange juice, milk, coffee or tea – and of course no alcohol!

The night before a game is also very important and I'd say that players should be 'early to bed'. A good night's sleep and plenty of relaxation before match day is vital at professional level and the early-to-bed rule never did me any harm when I was playing junior soccer.

Butterflies

You often hear people talking about pre-match nerves, and it's obvious that players do feel nervous before a game, no matter how much experience they might have had.

For a youngster playing his first competitive game there really is no reason to be nervous. I always say that you're playing soccer because you enjoy it. But it's still understandable. Just remember that there's a big difference between butterflies and panic!

Different players show their nerves in different ways, but for young players it's the excitement of the prospect of playing in the game which gives them the butterflies. This is nothing to be ashamed of, and once you get out on the field you quickly forget about any pre-match anxiety.

It's the same at top level. Even though players might feel a bit apprehensive before a game they quickly settle down and can soon find themselves enjoying things.

Look good, feel good

Appearance is another major factor to be considered. If you look smart on the field you'll look like a team.

We have a rule with England that players should always go out looking their best. They should be dressed properly, shirts tucked into their shorts, socks pulled up and tied so that they stay up, and most players run a comb through their hair before going onto the pitch. It's a matter of pride: we're proud to be playing for our country and we want to look the part.

I can't see any harm in junior clubs adopting the same attitude. If they go out looking like a team they'll soon learn to play like one.

Be prepared

At top clubs there are staff who are responsible for making sure that everybody has each piece of his kit ready on match day. Usually players look after their own boots, and by that I mean they clean the mud off them afterwards and make sure that they are properly polished and kept supple.

But at Manchester United, for example, we are lucky, our kit is put out for us on match days so that all we have to do is change into it and get on with the game!

Amateur clubs who provide shirts and shorts often expect players to get the kit washed and taken back to the club early the following week, and I think that this is a rule which should never be broken by players. Even if you're certain to be playing in the next game you're only letting the

Let's get on with it, then!

ROBSON'S TIPS

● *'Early to bed' should be the golden rule on the evening before a game. It doesn't do young players any harm to get plenty of rest before a match.*

● *Make sure that you eat a light meal before a game. Adults should not eat within three hours of a match and should stick to things like beans on toast, or scrambled eggs – but kids can eat anything!*

● *Drink as much liquid as you like before a game as you will burn it off during the match.*

● *Look smart when you go out on the field, with socks tied up properly and shirt tucked into your shorts. Don't look sloppy – there's no need for it and it doesn't impress anyone.*

---

side down if you don't adhere to the club rules, and there's nothing worse for a side that relies on its members than being let down by one of them being unprepared on match day.

A little time, a little thought and a lot of preparation make match days more enjoyable.

INJURIES AND TREATMENT

We've got all sorts of fancy equipment in our club physiotherapy rooms, but the most commonly used cure for bruises and muscle strains is ice. A pack of crushed ice will relieve pain from a bruise or a strain, and also help to heal the injury by restoring good circulation

It's obvious that in a contact sport like soccer players are going to get injured, especially since it's difficult to protect yourself completely. Surprisingly, injuries aren't as serious as they are in some other sports although the demand made on players at professional level does take its toll.

The most common injury is bruising, simply caused by players getting kicked by opponents. It's not easy for any player to go through a game without getting a few bumps and bruises, so I think that it's important for you to be able to understand something about injuries and how you should treat them.

Let me stress straight away that if a player is seriously injured he needs the correct treatment. This means seeing a doctor or a specialist who can diagnose the problem and give the right advice.

However, most of the knocks received during a game are those which can be dealt with simply, quickly and without a lot of fuss.

Ice work

It will probably come as a big surprise when I tell you that the most used piece of equipment in a soccer club's physio's treatment room is not the expensive electronic apparatus usually associated with such jobs, but ice. Yes, common or garden ice!

I must make it clear that you should never put ice directly onto the skin; it should always be in some sort of container. If you haven't got an ice-pack, use a rubber hot-water bottle or a plastic bag – anything that allows the ice to do its job without dripping all over the place when it starts to melt.

If you do put ice on your skin you'll do yourself more damage by 'burning', but applied properly ice will ease the pain in bruising and help to disperse the blood which gathers under the skin and gives the injury that black and blue appearance.

It's always best to use crushed ice, and you can break it up quite simply by wrapping cubes in a towel and either hitting them with a light hammer, or banging the towel onto a solid surface.

Clean cuts

Cuts are another minor injury associated with the game but because the game is usually played on grass, or surfaces which can leave dirt on a cut or a graze, it's important you make sure the cut is

ROBSON'S TIPS

● *A hot bath will get rid of aches and pains but you shouldn't lie in the bath if you have any fresh cuts or bruises. A shower is the best way of getting cuts clean after a game, but make sure that someone with medical experience sees your injury if there is any dirt close to it.*

● *You can make an ice-pack by putting crushed ice into a rubber hot-water bottle or a plastic bag. But never put the ice directly onto your flesh.*

● *Holding an ice-pack onto a bruise or strain for 10 minutes will disperse the blood and stop internal bleeding. Later, if ice is applied for 20 minutes it helps to restore good circulation.*

cleaned as quickly as possible.

This might mean nothing more than spending an extra few minutes under the shower bathing the cut. If a cut is deep it might require hospital treatment, and if there's much dirt in it it's always advisable to seek medical advice. There can always be complications.

Bathing cuts in warm water containing disinfectant is one way of making sure that they don't lead to any complications, and if they're covered with a clean dressing and perhaps some antiseptic cream this will also help. It's important that you don't neglect a cut, so I'd always advise young players to make sure they show the injury to a teacher, or their parents just to be safe. It's also a good idea to visit your doctor and have a course of injections against tetanus because you can be at risk if a cut or graze comes into contact with dirt or soil.

Aches and strains

A hot bath will always get rid of stiffness, but it isn't advisable to lie in a hot bath if you have any fresh cuts or bruises because this won't do them any good. A shower is much better, especially if the cut is still bleeding.

Younger players don't usually get the muscle strains and pulls which are quite common in

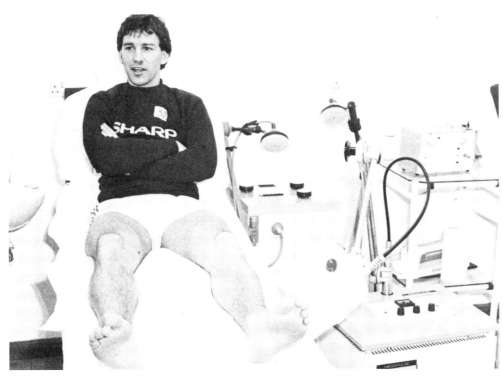

'older' players. But if you do the only real treatment is to apply ice packs regularly, and have plenty of rest.

Massage is another healer and is a good treatment for sore or tired muscles. It can also relieve pain if you get a kick on a fleshy part of the leg, like the calf or thigh.

Ice will disperse the internal bleeding, then after a couple of days' massage it's a good idea to apply ice again, this time leaving the pack on for about 20 minutes. This will help to improve the circulation in that area and this takes the pain away and restores the leg to full working order.

Once again I've got to make it clear that while it's possible to treat your own minor injuries it's always important that you take advice if you're worried that things aren't going the way they should.

Left: The Manchester United physiotherapy room at the club's training ground where the most modern equipment is used.

Below left: Bruises and strains can be treated by using a simple ice-pack. Here I am making a pack using a plastic bag and crushed ice.

Below right: Applying an ice-pack to a bruised toe. The ice eases the pain and helps to clear up bruise marks by improving circulation.

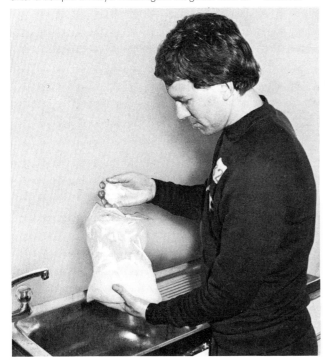

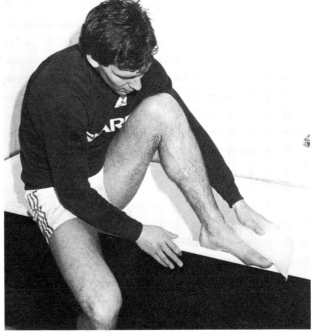

RETURNING AFTER INJURY

❝ I don't think I'm far off the mark when I say that around 75 per cent of top professional players can be carrying an injury. Such is the demand at the highest level that players have to play when they aren't quite ready, but they'll shrug off the effects and get on with the game. It's only when you're totally immobilized with a strain or break that you have to stand down. So it's a risky business **❞**

Most players find themselves getting back to the game after being out through injury at some stage of their careers, and it's very important that they go about things the right way. Expert advice is necessary, especially in the case of a serious injury which may have kept you out for several weeks or even months.

If you have broken a leg and been out of action for a long period it's vital that you see an experienced physiotherapist before taking up the game again, and that you don't return too quickly.

After such a break the standard treatment is some kind of physiotherapy at the local hospital. It may not be the kind of rehabilitation you'd get if you were a professional player but it'll help you to get the full use of your leg again after it's been in plaster for six weeks or so.

One of the first areas you have to work on is the ankle joint, because this will have stiffened if it has been encased in a plaster cast. Cycling, skipping and gentle step-up exercises are invaluable and they will also help to restore waste muscle.

Your leg will be weaker so you must not try to play any kind of soccer right away.

Take your time
The motto of every young player trying to get back to full fitness after a serious injury must be to *take your time*. It's a slow, frustrating process, but if you rush things then you can create much bigger problems for yourself later on, as well as putting yourself back to square one again.

After you feel the strength returning to your leg and you're confident that you've got the correct amount of movement in it, that's the time to start kicking a ball about. Nothing too heavy, just light practice at first, increasing slowly in time and power as the days go by. Again, take it easy.

You may decide to go along to the training sessions at your local club, but I'd advise you to be selective. Just join in the kickabout; then with a pal perhaps work your way up to trying a few passes; then get him to hold the ball while you try to win it from him.

The first tackle you make after breaking your leg will be a test of your confidence, and once you realize that you can do it you'll find that other areas of your game will quickly return too.

Time is the best healer
Walking, light jogging and then general running all add to your fitness and strength, and you must always remember that the best healer is your own body. You have a built-in self-restoring system which will work for you if you let it, and get plenty of sensible exercise. Make sure that your circulation is working well through plenty of massage, hot baths and ice application on stiff muscles.

One important thing to note is that if you get any pain at all when doing exercises following a break you must go and see your physio-therapist. Once the original stiffness has gone after your leg has been released from the plaster you shouldn't have any pain, just a bit of stiffness because your muscles tire easily.

I'd say that the normal return period after having the cast removed from a broken leg or ankle is about four or five weeks. You work your way up to normal running and exercise by progressing through walking, half-running, jogging, and so on.

Keep off the weights
Never do any weight training immediately after a break. Only use weights when you have some strength back in the leg, and even then you must use only the lightest ones at first.

While broken bones in other parts of your body might not be too pleasant they won't cause you the same kind of problems leg or ankle breaks will, at least as far as soccer is concerned. But they should be treated in the same way, building up flexibility, mobility and strength gradually.

Next down in the injury league table probably will be dislocations, and I can speak from plenty of experience when I say that these are quite painful! Here again time is the healer, once the initial injury has been treated by the medical experts. You need to strengthen muscles around the trouble-spot, and this is a gradual process.

Serious cuts will mean you missing games, but it's possible to play with dressings covering minor gashes. I have actually played with stitches in wounds and had no problems, yet there are times when I've had smaller cuts in different areas which have meant me being out.

Psychological factors
When you do get back into the game you have to overcome the psychological pressures of taking part in a soccer match again. You will always have it in the back of your mind that if you do the same thing again you will get hurt once more. The chances are very slim that you'll pick up the same injury, but it can take time to convince someone who has been hurt that this is the case.

The long road back to fitness. I jog alone as I build back my strength after being out of the game through injury.

It's at moments like this that you have to decide for yourself. People can advise you as much as they like, and even though I can tell you that I've gone through it all this means nothing: it's your decision.

All I can say is that there are thousands of top players who have played the game over many years who have come back after serious injury and continued their careers. There are also a great many who have been injured before they made it to the top and have managed to overcome this obstacle and still reach the professional level of the game.

If that's your ambition then you'll have to convince yourself that a little bit of pain isn't going to stand in your way.

There will come a moment during a game when your injury – or the part of your body which had been injured – is put to the test. It might be the first slide tackle you make in serious competition three months after breaking your ankle; it may be the first real challenge since you broke a leg; or a heading duel a few weeks after that nasty gash. But when you've come through it unscathed you'll wonder why you worried in the first place!

ROBSON'S TIPS

● *Always see a doctor or medical adviser before playing after a serious injury.*

● *Don't rush it: give yourself time to recover from an injury. If you're not fully fit you're taking a major risk that you'll hurt yourself again – and spend even longer out of the game.*

● *After breaking a leg or ankle, build up flexibility and strength before you start working with the ball.*

● *When you return to training for the first time after a break don't do any work that could involve physical contact – even accidental contact.*

FINDING A CLUB

❝ When I was at school a few of my pals played for a local junior team on Saturday afternoons. They asked me to go along as well and the manager said that I could have a couple of games to see how I got on. Eventually I signed and used to play for the school on a Saturday morning, and then for the junior team in the afternoon. I loved my football then . . . and I still do ❞

Wherever I go one of the most frequent questions I get asked is: 'How do you become a footballer?' It's actually very easy to answer, even though the way to the top level in soccer is quite difficult.

My answer is simply to keep working at your game and the chances will come. I know that may sound a little casual, as if I was dismissing the question, but truthfully the only way that you'll ever succeed in football is by hard work.

The road to the top is straightforward enough. You begin at school level, then perhaps get selected for your town or city area team. The next step is to play for your county, still at school level, and the pinnacle of a youngster's game is to represent his country. That's putting it very simply, I know, and if you're looking for a way to get on in the game don't think that I've just described the blueprint for success.

Cubs and clubs

Let's start at the beginning. You enjoy playing football and most of your spare time is spent with a group of your pals kicking a ball about. Well, my first question for you is: 'Where is the nearest team which caters for youngsters of your age?'

The answer is probably at school, or the local church, or perhaps the scout or cubs group. Yes, that's where I started my competitive career – in the cubs!

I enjoyed playing at school but wanted a bit more from the game, and one of my pals was in the cubs. He told me that they had a good football team and said that because I was already playing for the school I would probably go straight into the cub team if I enrolled.

I've got to confess that I had no real interest in the cubs or scouting when I joined, but I wanted to play football and they had a team. As it turned out they had reached the quarter-finals of the local junior cup competition and I went straight into the team; we reached the final and won!

Sometimes youngsters will form their own team if they have enough pals to get 12 or 13 players turning out regularly, and they can go as far as joining a league themselves. Ask your parents or teacher about them. There are hundreds of examples of this sort of thing happening, and when I tell you that one club formed by a group of railway workers went on to change its name to Manchester United you'll see what I mean!

Being 'discovered'

Until a youngster reaches the age of about 12 he has no real reason to take his football too seriously. Once he's started senior school, if he has ambitions to become a footballer he must set his sights on getting into the school team.

Most schools have more than one team, each catering for different age groups, but it's usually the under-13 team which catches the eye of the top clubs.

They have scouts who watch the games regularly and will note any promising players. The normal process is for the scout to invite the youngster along to the club he represents, usually in the school holidays. He'll always approach the youngster through his teacher or his parents – never directly.

Once a scout from one club has made it known that he's looking at a particular player it's surprising where the others come from! It's quite common for a young player to get several invitations to visit clubs, even though he may not be 14 yet.

This happened to me and I chose West Bromwich Albion as the club I wanted to train with during the summer. I enjoyed going there, training with a group of about 30 youngsters, all of the same age.

We were still at school but all of us wanted to be footballers, and we had signed a form to say that we wouldn't go to another club without notifying West Brom. Eventually I was taken on as an apprentice, and then became a professional. Of course not every youngster who plays football is that lucky to be good enough and get the chance to take up the game professionally. There are youngsters who want to play but have their minds set on other careers. This shouldn't stop you from enjoying your football.

There are some very good youth club teams, works teams and good standards of football played at college and university, so there's no reason why anyone who wants to play football at a decent level should go without a game, provided he's good enough to get into a team.

Summer coaching courses

A lot of youngsters nowadays go along to the summer coaching courses run by ex-professional players and use them as the first step towards a career in the game. The soccer schools take youngsters in a holiday atmosphere and give them lessons in skills and tactics. They organize matches and provide coaching and advice sessions to bring out the best in their pupils. I know from personal experience that two of the

The first steps to professional soccer. Here I am with the rest of my pals in the Cub team which won the Chester-le-Street District Association Cup in 1967. I've got to confess that I joined the Cubs because of the soccer team, but I don't think anyone minded! That's me second from the right on the front row.

youngsters I've spoken to when I've visited one of the major schools have gone on to join Manchester United and Tottenham, so this is certainly a way of getting into the game.

So while school team to football club is the normal direct path, there are other ways.

Players like Gary Bailey and Craig Johnston asked English clubs to give them a trial when they lived overseas and proved good enough to be offered contracts, and you regularly read stories about players who have been plucked out of non-League football and taken on by League clubs.

Work hard, play hard

Once a player becomes a professional his life has to be totally dedicated to the game. If he doesn't enjoy playing an average of two matches every week throughout a season, training each day and having to maintain a standard of fitness to give him the stamina to last a whole game and not be overtired, then he just won't survive.

I have emphasized time and again in this book that you have to enjoy your football, whether it's the cub team hoping to reach the second round of their local cup competition, or the world champions going out to defend their trophy. If the players aren't loving every moment of the game, they're not going to give their best.

Playing at any level demands concentration, skill, determination and effort, and if you always give 100 per cent you'll enjoy being part of the team . . . of any team.

ROBSON'S TIPS

● *Most people get into football through their friends. There's bound to be a team in your area which caters for youngsters of your age and will offer you the chance to play. And if there isn't, form one with your pals!*

● *The first ambition of any would-be footballer must be to get into his school team. From there he'll get the chance to move up the ladder.*

● *Soccer schools provide players with the chance to test their ability against others, and if you're good enough you will get the chance to prove it.*

● *If you do get invited to join a professional club, go to one which is well organized and which looks after its young players – not necessarily the club you support.*

ROBSON'S CAREER HIGHLIGHTS

From a cub scout soccer team to the captaincy of England and Manchester United: that is the road to soccer stardom taken by Bryan Robson.

Like many small boys in Britain, Bryan began playing soccer almost as soon as he could run around. A beach holiday with his parents, a game in the garden, then off to the local park with his schoolmates and a ball. Wherever he went Bryan Robson loved to kick a ball.

At school he began to show promise and eventually played his first representative game, for Chester-le-Street Juniors, captaining the team in the 1967–68 season.

Soon people in soccer began to take notice of young Bryan and he was given the chance to join West Bromwich Albion as a schoolboy – the club agreeing to coach the youngster during his holidays, Bryan guaranteeing that he would not join another club without their permission.

As soon as he left school he was destined for the top. He joined West Brom as a young professional in August 1974 and by the end of that first season was drafted into the first team for the closing three games of the season – and scored in two of them.

He was selected to play for England at youth level and showed his versatility for West Bromwich in his second season when he played in just 14 games but in six different positions ranging from full-back to centre-forward and at times in the centre of defence and midfield.

Injury hit the start of his career and three times he broke his ankle but he showed the determination which in later years was to be even more evident, by fighting his way back and finally becoming the most sought-after player in Britain.

He showed that he had a knack of scoring important goals, never more so than in his first full season, when at Bolton he scored the winner in a victory for West Brom. At the end of the season West Brom were promoted after finishing third in the Second Division league table – one point ahead of Bolton.

He soon became recognized as an outstanding player with West Brom and was selected for the England Under-21 side. In 1980 he made his full international debut against the Republic of Ireland and the following year, when he was transferred to Manchester United for a record fee of £1.5 million, he was established as a regular in the national team.

He scored five goals for United in his first season, doubling this figure the following year and taking over the captaincy of both club and country after an injury to his United colleague Ray Wilkins.

Bryan led United to FA Cup victories against Brighton in 1983 and Everton in 1985, and has played in two World Cups for England, scoring the fastest goal of the tournament in 1982 in just 27 seconds in the opening game against France. He missed most of the 1986 campaign because of a dislocated shoulder which later required surgery.

Tom Tyrrell

GLOSSARY

Aerial combat Competition between two or more players from opposing sides to make contact with the ball when it is in the air.

Attacker Forward player whose role is to penetrate the opposing defence.

Back four The four defenders at the rear of a team made up of two full-backs and two centre-backs.

Back heel A method of kicking, using the heel to project the ball to the rear or side.

Ball control Keeping the ball within good contact distance and being able to prevent it from rolling beyond reach.

Bicycle kick An acrobatic kick when the player makes contact with the ball while his feet are at the highest point of a back somersault. The action is similar to that used when lying on the floor with legs raised in a 'cycling' exercise.

Centre To cross the ball by kicking it from the wing into the middle of the field of play.

Centre-back A defensive position in the back four. Teams normally have two centre-backs, one playing to the right, the other to the left. They form the centre of the defence.

Centre circle The circle marked in the middle of the halfway line. At kick-off or when play is being restarted members of the opposing team are not allowed to enter the circle until the ball has been kicked forward by the side in possession.

Centre-forward The striker who leads the attack.

Chip To kick the ball into the air with a stabbing movement of the foot. This method is often used to project the ball over an advancing goalkeeper or a defensive wall.

Crossbar The horizontal bar which rests on the two goalposts to form a goal.

Dead ball When a ball is placed on the ground for a player to kick it is described as being 'dead', as opposed to a moving ball. Also when the ball has crossed the goal-line after being played by a member of the attacking side it is 'dead' until brought back into play from a goalkick.

Defender Players whose role it is to prevent the opposition from penetrating their half of the field and to defend their goal.

Defensive wall The group of players who form a barrier between the ball and their goal when a free kick has been awarded within scoring distance.

Direct free kick A free kick from which a goal can be scored, awarded for a foul or handling offence outside the penalty area.

'Doggies' Shuttle-running exercises used in training when players sprint from a starting line to markers set at short distances. Running to a marker, turning and running back to the start line simulates sprinting during actual play.

Dribble To try to beat an opponent by tricking him with close ball control and deceptive movements of the feet.

Foul An infringement of the rules when a player has been adjudged by the referee to have intentionally kicked, tripped or pushed an opponent.

Free kick The method of starting play after an infringement.

Full-back The defender on either side of the back four whose role is to prevent attacking players from penetrating down the flank.

Goal The object of the game, to score a goal. This is achieved when the whole of the ball crosses the goal-line either on or above the ground and between the two upright and one horizontal bar. The construction of posts and net is also known as the goal.

Goal area The rectangle within the penalty area from which goalkicks are taken.

Goalkeeper The player who defends the goal. He can handle the ball within the penalty area.

Goalkick The method of restarting play after the ball has crossed the goal-line, not between the posts, after being last played by a member of the attacking side.

Goal-line The line which runs from corner flag to corner flag across each end of the field of play and on which the goal is situated.

Half-volley Kicking the ball as it makes contact with the ground after either dropping it from the hand (in the case of a goalkeeper) or from a lofted kick.

Handball An offence, if a player other than a goalkeeper is adjudged by the referee to have intentionally played the ball with his hand or arm. If a defender handles within the penalty area a penalty is given, if a goalkeeper handles the ball outside the penalty area a direct free kick is awarded.

Indirect A free kick from which a goal cannot be scored by the player taking the kick, unless the ball touches or is played by another from either side. Indirect free kicks are awarded for obstruction within or outside the penalty area.

Inside foot The flat area between the inner ankle bone, heel and big toe which is used for accurate low kicks.

Instep The area of the foot in a line along the big toe towards the ankle and the most used kicking area in football.

Linesman The official – there are two for each match – who assists the referee and patrols each touchline to indicate when a ball is out of play or a player is offside.

Marking To cover an opponent and prevent him from gaining an advantageous position.

Midfield The position played by creative members of the team whose role is to link attack and defence.

Offside An infringement, when a player from the attacking side plays the ball forward to a colleague who doesn't have two opponents beyond him and the goal his side is attacking. A player can be offside only in the opposition half of the field.

Passing Kicking the ball to a colleague or into an area which enables a team mate to collect it without interception from the opposition.

Penalty The free kick (direct) awarded for a foul or intentional handball within the penalty area.

Penalty area The larger of the two rectangles which surround the goal.

Referee The official in charge of a game. It is his responsibility to enforce the laws of the game and act as timekeeper.

Scissor kick Kicking the ball when both feet are off the ground either in an upright or horizontal position and when the kicker's legs cross in a cutting action as contact is made.

Striker The centre-forward or attacking player whose role is to score goals.

Sweeper The defender commonly used by teams from mainland Europe to play behind the back four and support both defensive and attacking play.

Tackle To challenge an opponent who is in possession and try to win the ball.

Throw-in The method of restarting play when the ball has crossed the touchline. A throw-in is awarded to the opposing side to that which last touched the ball before it went out of play.

Tie-up The short piece of bandage, or similar material, used for holding up a player's socks.

Touchline The line running the full length of the field on each side of the playing aea.

Upright The name given to the goalposts which support the crossbar.

Volley To kick the ball while it is off the ground.

Wall pass To play the ball to a colleague and run forward to receive a return pass around an opponent.

Winger The player on the left or right side of the attack whose role is to play close to the touchline.

INDEX